Concurrency Control and Recovery in OLTP Systems

High Scalability and Availability

East China Normal University Scientific Reports
Subseries on Data Science and Engineering

ISSN: 2382-5715

Chief Editor
Weian Zheng
Changjiang Chair Professor
School of Finance and Statistics
East China Normal University, China
Email: financialmaths@gmail.com

Associate Chief Editor
Shanping Wang
Senior Editor
Journal of East China Normal University (Natural Sciences), China
Email: spwang@library.ecnu.edu.cn

This book series reports valuable research results and progress in scientific and related areas. Mainly contributed by the distinguished professors of the East China Normal University, it will cover a number of research areas in pure mathematics, financial mathematics, applied physics, computer science, environmental science, geography, estuarine and coastal science, education information technology, etc.

Published

Vol. 9 *Concurrency Control and Recovery in OLTP Systems: High Scalability and Availability*
by Peng Cai (East China Normal University, China),
Jinwei Guo (East China Normal University, China) and
Aoying Zhou (East China Normal University, China)

Vol. 8 *Network Data Mining and Analysis*
by Ming Gao (East China Normal University, China),
Ee-Peng Lim (Singapore Management University, Singapore) and
David Lo (Singapore Management University, Singapore)

Vol. 7 *Time-Aware Conversion Prediction for E-Commerce*
by Wendi Ji (East China Normal University, China),
Xiaoling Wang (East China Normal University, China) and
Aoying Zhou (East China Normal University, China)

More information on this series can also be found at https://www.worldscientific.com/series/ecnusr

(Continued at end of book)

East China Normal University Scientific Reports | Vol. 9
Subseries on Data Science and Engineering

Concurrency Control and Recovery in OLTP Systems

High Scalability and Availability

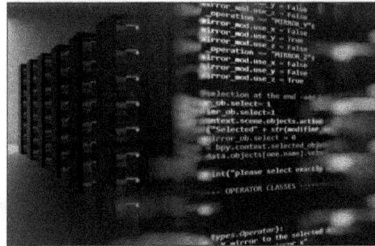

Peng Cai

Jinwei Guo

Aoying Zhou

East China Normal University, China

World Scientific

NEW JERSEY · LONDON · SINGAPORE · BEIJING · SHANGHAI · HONG KONG · TAIPEI · CHENNAI · TOKYO

Published by

World Scientific Publishing Co. Pte. Ltd.

5 Toh Tuck Link, Singapore 596224

USA office: 27 Warren Street, Suite 401-402, Hackensack, NJ 07601

UK office: 57 Shelton Street, Covent Garden, London WC2H 9HE

Library of Congress Cataloging-in-Publication Data

Names: Cai, Peng, author. | Guo, Jinwei, author. | Zhou, Aoying, 1965–   author.

Title: Concurrency control and recovery in OLTP systems : high scalability and availability /
    by Peng Cai (East China Normal University, China), Jinwei Guo (East China Normal University,
    China) and Aoying Zhou (East China Normal University, China).

Description: New Jersey : World Scientific, [2019] | Series: East China Normal University
    scientific reports ; volume 9 | Includes bibliographical references.

Identifiers: LCCN 2019005899| ISBN 9789813279223 (hc : alk. paper) |
    ISBN 9789813279230 (pbk : alk. paper)

Subjects: LCSH: Transaction systems (Computer systems) | Online data processing. |
    Database management.

Classification: LCC QA76.545 .C35 2019 | DDC 005.74/5--dc23

LC record available at https://lccn.loc.gov/2019005899

British Library Cataloguing-in-Publication Data

A catalogue record for this book is available from the British Library.

For any available supplementary material, please visit
https://www.worldscientific.com/worldscibooks/10.1142/11242#t=suppl

Desk Editors: Herbert Moses/Amanda Yun

Typeset by Stallion Press
Email: enquiries@stallionpress.com

East China Normal University Scientific Reports

Preface

Transaction is one of important concepts in database systems, and its digestible ACID properties provide a wonderful guide for database implementation. Concurrency control and recovery are two key mechanisms for transaction processing. Despite the success of database products in business markets, recent development of hardware techniques and new requirements from emerging applications require database architecture to be redesigned. As the memory size of the commodity server continues to increase and its cost also continues to decrease, the working data set of most applications can be fully held in main-memory database systems. The overhead of traditional disk-based database systems, including buffer management and disk I/O, has disappeared. The left cost of modern OLTP systems comes mainly from concurrency control and log processing.

Multi-version Storage Engine. Multi-version concurrency control is a popular concurrency control protocol owing to its amazing property—read and write are not necessary to block each other. In the setting of main-memory OLTP systems, the main cost of MVCC is to find the available and specified version for a running transaction. The commonly used storage formats have two types. The first is to use a linked list to store a record with its versions from the oldest to the latest. The second is to link versions from the latest to the oldest. However, both of these storage schemes have disadvantages under different access patterns. In the second chapter, we introduce an optimized storage format which stores the latest two versions in the head of a linked list. This kind of MVCC storage scheme can avoid the problem of point chasing for read and write operations.

Range Concurrency Control. Many applications from industries in finance, e-commerce and Internet of Things are driven by their collected transactional data. These applications require database systems not only to handle traditional transactions which include read and write operations with primary or secondary keys, but also to process analytical transactions mixed point queries and key-range scan queries for aggregate operations. These kinds of workloads are termed as Hybrid Transaction and Analytical Processing (HTAP). We present an efficient optimistic concurrency control for workloads with key-range scan operations in the third chapter.

Global Snapshot Isolation. Snapshot isolation (SI) is a practical isolation level implemented in many commercial or open-source database systems. Global snapshot isolation is to provide the same semantics of SI in a Paxos-replicated database system. As an isolation level, SI is stronger than read committed and comparable to repeatable read. We assume a main-memory database can be held by a single machine and fully replicated by other machines. One of these machines is elected as leader, and the others are regarded as followers. In the fourth chapter, we design and implement an efficient implementation of global snapshot isolation.

Log Replication. Replication techniques can improve the performance and availability of database systems. The asynchronous primary-backup replication has been widely implemented and deployed in most database systems. As a general technique, replication is also an important research topic in distributed system community. In recent years, consensus (e.g., Paxos and Raft)-based replication protocols have been taken as the first choice of replicating data among different machines. We will present an efficient quorum-based replication for main-memory database systems in the fifth chapter.

Follower Recovery. Although a Raft group is able to provide services when a majority of machine members are available, it would be helpful for the high availability and read scalability of system if the crashed member can be recovered quickly. When a Raft replicated follower database node is crashed, it needs to synchronize local logs with the master node and can then rejoin the Raft group. This procedure of log synchronization consists of two steps. The first is to delete uncommitted logs, and the second is to copy the missing committed logs from the leader database node. In the sixth chapter, we introduce a fast follower recovery scheme, which reduces the network overhead of log synchronization.

About the Authors

Peng Cai is an Associate Professor in the School of Data Science and Engineering at East China Normal University (ECNU). He received his PhD degree in Computer Science and Technology from ECNU in 2011. He joined ECNU in 2015, prior to which Peng worked for the IBM China Research Lab and Baidu. His work has been published in various leading conferences, such as ICDE, SIGIR and ACL. His main research interests include in-memory transaction processing and building adaptive systems using machine learning techniques.

Jinwei Guo is a PhD candidate in the School of Data Science and Engineering at ECNU. He received his bachelor's degree in Computer Science and Technology from Qufu Normal University, China in 2010, and his master's degree from Guizhou University, China in 2014. His research interests include transaction processing in database management systems (DBMS) and high availability in distributed systems.

Aoying Zhou is currently the Vice President of ECNU and a Professor in the School of Data Science and Engineering. He received his master's and bachelor's degrees in Computer Science from Sichuan University, China in 1988 and 1985, respectively, and his PhD degree from Fudan University, China in 1993. Before joining ECNU in 2008, Aoying worked for Fudan University in the Computer Science Department for 15 years. He is the winner of the National Science Fund for Distinguished Young Scholars supported by the National Natural Science Foundation of China (NSFC), as well as the professorship appointment under the Changjiang Scholars Program of the Ministry of Education, China. He is now acting as the Vice Director of Association for Computing Machinery's Special Interest Group on Management of Data (ACM SIGMOD), China and the Database Technology Committee of the China Computer Federation. Prof Zhou was a serving member of the editorial boards of journals such as *The VLDB Journal* and *World Wide Web Journal* among others. His research interests include web data management, data management for data-intensive computing, memory cluster computing, benchmarking for big data and performance.

Contents

List of Figures

List of Tables

1

Introduction

1.1 Background

Online transaction processing (OLTP) systems have become the core component of IT infrastructure in modern enterprise for several decades, and they have been widely deployed in many industries such as finance, telecommunication, e-commerce, etc. The IBM System-R project, beginning in 1974[a], still has an influence on the system architecture and implementation of most traditional OLTP systems. Compared with computing environment in the past four decades, there has been huge progress in CPU, storage and network techniques. The cost of RAM continues to decrease, and the machine with large memory can hold the whole working set for OLTP applications. As it is difficult to improve the performance of a single core in CPU, multi-core processors are invented to increase computing power. However, if there are no adjustments to the system design of OLTP systems, we cannot make full use of the power from new hardware technology.

The new application scenario has created a big challenge to the traditional OLTP systems. In recent years, we have witnessed the proliferation of smartphones in people's daily lives. With the prevalence of mobile applications and 4G networks, people can access what they want at anytime and from anywhere. With smartphones, a user can reach the service at any time and trigger the back-end system to start a

---

[a]Ibm db2. https://en.wikipedia.org/wiki/IBM_DB2/.

transaction processing for buying tickets, online shopping, stock trading, etc. In these applications, OLTP systems must be equipped with the ability of continuous service because Internet users may access the system at any time. The shutdown of system services would lose many users, which means the revenue is also reduced. In a nutshell, most enterprise applications or services should consider how to provide flexible and stable transaction processing for uncertain number of users. In the setting of a cluster with many commodity servers, an OLTP system must have horizontal scalability, and also guarantee reliability and availability.

Traditional OLTP systems often host on the single machine or multiple machines with large share storage such as Storage Area Networks (SANs) and Network Attached Storage (NAS). The system designers consider these hardwares as sufficiently reliable and fault events rarely happen, and OLTP systems mainly depend on expensive hardware to provide the high availability. To enhance the throughput of transaction processing, the common choice is to replace the original hardware with more advanced and high-end hardware. In addition to hardware upgrade, deploying a new version of OLTP software or fixing bugs also requires the system to shut down and stop the service for several hours or days. Generally speaking, these procedures require the database administrators (DBA) or system vendors to make a more detailed plan for each step, and although much effort has been taken, it still proves to be full of risk. However, we will consider it is unimaginable if the online shopping websites can not serve the user request. In a word, today's Internet users have been accustomed to enjoying shopping at any time.

The emergence of plenty of NoSQL systems aims to meet these requirements. Therefore, these systems have been widely used in Internet applications such as social media and web content caching [13]. Although NoSQL systems have better scalability and performance, many virtues in traditional OLTP systems have been removed. Especially, NoSQL systems offer weak support for transaction processing and ACID properties are not fully supported. This may lead to that the application programmer having to do much work on the problem of data inconsistency resulting from concurrent operations over data store. Furthermore, for the mission-critical applications, they need not only the ability of scale-out similar to NoSQL systems but also strong support of full ACID. Therefore, the next generation of OLTP systems has been proposed and implemented, referred to as NewSQL systems. To achieve new features such as scale-out ability, active upgrade and fault tolerance over commodity machines, the NewSQL systems should redesign the whole architecture. Concurrency control and recovery as the most important components in OLTP systems have been revisited and redesigned.

1.2 New OLTP Architectures

New OLTP systems have optimized the design of most key components such as storage, logging and concurrency control. Their architectures provide unique features that are different from traditional DBMSs. In this section, we classify these systems according to how the database is partitioned and concurrent transactions are executed.

The first kind of OLTP systems partition the whole database and distribute the data in multiple nodes. The design goal of these systems is to scale out the capability of transaction processing by adding more computing nodes. The design philosophy of H-Store was proposed in VLDB 2007 by Michael Stonebraker *et al.* [89]. In the original prototype of H-Store, each partition can held in memory, which indicates no disk latency during transaction execution. Furthermore, H-Store requires that all codes of each transaction are submitted at once. This feature means it does't need to wait user input and there is no network latency between the client and OLTP server. Since there is no latency from disk, network and user input, there is no need to parallelize the transaction processing over a single partition. In H-Store, each partition is accessed by a single thread, and if there are no cross-partition transactions, the throughput can be linearly scaled out with the number of cores or nodes. For the transactions over local partition, there are no concurrent control schemes because the local transactions are executed one by one. For the cross-partition transactions, H-Store adopted a two-phase commit protocol [29] to coordinate the execution procedure among different partition nodes.

Although partition and replication are the main approaches to horizontally scale the throughput of transaction processing, the high cost of distributed transaction using 2PC is prohibitive in the application where the database cannot be well partitioned. CalvinDB considers the dynamic locking scheme is the root cause of high-cost concurrency control. Thus, it reduces the cost of executing distributed transaction using deterministic concurrent control strategy. The architecture of CalvinDB comprises three layers. Before executing transactions, CalvinDB collects the inputs of incoming transaction requests at the sequencing layer. This layer determines the serialization order of transactions, and all replicas follow this order. The second layer, called scheduling layer, orchestrates the transaction execution using deterministic locking method. Storage layer is the third layer for physical data layout and provides the CRUD interface.

Different from most cluster-based OLTP systems where each machine is the owner of some partitions, Hyder doesn't partition the database and locally stores the whole database snapshot at each machine. There is a shared log component to collect update information from different machines, and the local snapshot is freshened using a log melding component. This log meld procedure is conducted on each machine to ensure the update operations are applied in the same order. As each transaction can access all data from the local snapshot, Hyder circumvents the problem of distributed transaction.

Generally speaking, the transaction processing model and data access method are tightly bounded in the implementation of traditional OLTP systems. The architecture of Deuteronomy separates the transaction processing function from data access and storage component. Its main motivation is to scale the performance by adding more storage nodes or transaction processing nodes. However, this architecture leads to some challenges for concurrency control because concurrent transactions don't know which records really exist in the database before they get the returned results from the storage layer.

Compared to traditional centralized DBMSs, key-value systems (say Cassandra, HBase, Redis, etc.) have advantages such as low latency, scalability and high availability, and many of them have been widely adopted in many industry projects. These systems achieve high performance by sacrificing the ACID properties. However, due to the lack of support for transaction processing, the programmer must take much effort to consider the concurrent conflicts. Therefore, this motivates the need to equip the transaction processing function with key-value systems. Both Percolator and Omid belong to this kind of OLTP systems and they can support cross-row and cross-table transactions. Percolator is built on Google's Bigtable, which only supports single row transaction, and it stores locking information with the data and uses two-phase commit protocol to coordinate the distributed transactions. Omid has a transaction manager component that is independent of the bottom storage layer HBase, which is regarded as the open source implementation of Bigtable.

OceanBase (OB), developed by Alibaba, partitions the database according to whether the data is being updated. OB uses a single update server (UPS) to store the active data which are being updated by transactions, and the static data are distributed and replicated on many chunk servers (CSs). This design is based on the observation that the size of updated data during a fixed time (e.g., one day) is limited in most OLTP settings. When the used memory of UPS is beyond the defined threshold, OB merges the active data from the UPS to CSs. This architecture has the advantage of avoiding distributed transactions because all update transactions are running on a single UPS. OB provides the high availability by log replication between primary UPS and backup UPS. To reduce the workload of primary UPS, read-only transactions can be routed to backup UPS.

1.3 Concurrency Control

Transaction is one of the most important concepts in OLTP systems. In real applications, it often defines certain business behaviors such as transfering money from one account to another account, buying a ticket, making a new order, etc. One transaction often consists of a sequence of operations over data objects, and OLTP systems can interleave the execution of operations from different transactions. However, without appropriate concurrency control, the interleaving of executing operations from different transactions will result in all kinds of problems, including dirty read, lost update, non-repeatable read, etc. To resolve the problem from concurrently executing transactions, concurrency control scheme has been the hot topic in the past decades and becomes the key component in OLTP systems. Generally speaking, it aims to guarantee the data consistency on the one hand, and to coordinate as many transactions as possible that can be concurrently executed on the other hand. To guarantee the correctness of the database, each transaction should obey the ACID rule, i.e., Atomicity, Consistency, Isolation and Durability. In order to achieve this goal, three kinds of concurrency control schemes have been proposed in the database research community. They are two-phase locking (2PL), optimistic concurrency control and timestamp ordering, respectively.

Locking is the most widely implemented and deployed concurrency control mechanism in so many commercial or open-source DBMSs including DB2, ORACLE, MySQL, PostgreSQL, etc. The well-known 2PL protocol schedules the potential data access conflicts in the pessimistic way. All lock requests happen at the first phase, where the transaction would firstly lock the record or a set of records before it reads or updates the data. The transaction enters the second phase if one lock is released and then lock requests are disallowed. Furthermore, to ensure the serializable schedule, strict 2PL protocol requires the locks be held by a transaction to be released after this transaction is committed.

Under optimistic concurrency control [53], the lifetime of each transaction is divided into three phases, i.e., read, validation and write phase. In the first phase, each transaction only tentatively writes data in the local version and essentially doesn't feel the existence of other transactions. Before the transaction commits, validation phase is used to detect whether there are conflicts with other committed and lifetime-overlapped transactions. If the validation fails, the transaction being validated will be aborted. Although all kinds of methods about pessimistic or optimistic schemes have been proposed, there is no method that always performs better than all other methods. In the setting with high conflicts, locking-based pessimistic method has better performance over optimistic method. However, if the applications only have lower conflicts, optimistic method performs better.

As the hardware techniques have made great progress and the scenario of OLTP application continues to evolve and differentiates from that in last several 10 years, both pessimistic and optimistic methods have been revisited and received much attention from the research community.

In the following, we summarize some related work on how to optimize the implementation in the setting of multiple cores and how to adapt existing concurrency control schemes to modern OLTP application.

The traditional implementation of 2PL protocol has a locking manager component which adopts the hash map as the central data structure shared by multiple threads. In the hash map, a key represents a locked item, and its value is often a linked list which stores the information of transaction holding this lock and those transactions waiting for the lock release. It is reported that the cost of locking overhead takes nearly up to 16–25%. To reduce the locking overhead and improve the scalability of locking algorithm under multi-core machine, existing works give up central data structure and co-allocate locking information with raw data items. Especially for the hot data item, frequent locking acquisition and release leads to expensive memory allocation and deallocation. Lock inheritance resolves this problem by transferring the allocated lock information to another transaction. In Section 2.2, we introduce more related works on locking.

As read and write operations don't block each other in multiple version concurrency control (MVCC), it has received much more attention in recent years. Snapshot isolation based on MVCC has been implemented in most DBMS products including SQL Server, Oracle, PostgreSQL, etc. Although snapshot isolation level has removed the most abnormal phenomena, it is still possible to generate non-serializable transaction execution because of write skew problem. The write skew problem happens when two transactions read the same set of records but they modify different records in this set. While it seems that each of two transactions obeys the consistency constraints, the final state of the database is inconsistent. Serializable snapshot isolation was proposed to resolve the write skew problem. The key idea is to track the read and write set of each running transaction, and then to build run-time dependency graph. If there exists a cycle in the dependency graph, the write skew problem will occur. However, it would take much cost to detect write skew problem. This is because maintaining all access records of each running transaction is a resource-intensive task. The authors of Ref. [79] introduced an approximate solution of keeping rw-dependency in-conflicts and out-conflicts for each transaction. If the transaction is dependent on by other transactions and it also depends on another transactions, it means this is the joint transaction. Thus, it is possible there is a dependency cycle. As the existence of the joint transaction does not mean it absolutely has a dependency cycle, this results of detection may be false positive.

1.4 Crash Recovery

OLTP systems must provide the ability to avoid data loss or inconsistency in case of unpredictable failures including transaction abort, disk corrupt, OS crash, etc. The recovery mechanism of OLTP aims to guarantee the atomicity and durability of the ACID properties [33]. By this mechanism, each transaction has its corresponding committed log which contains all details of update operations. Write-Ahead Logging (WAL) is the widely used logging protocol whose key idea is that the transaction log must be flushed to persistent storage before committing the transaction [11]. When OLTP systems crash for some reasons, the latest commited data in the volatile memory will be lost since these data have perhaps not been flushed to non-volatile media. By replaying the committed log, the database can be recovered to the moment when the system crashes, and then all committed data are available.

Traditional database systems often rely on high-end expensive hardware to provide the high availability, and these systems regard hardware faults as abnormal events. To achieve the ability of fast recovery from system crash, conventional database systems adopt replication techniques to copy transaction log from primary DBMS instance to backup instance. When the primary node is shut down because of failures, the backup node switches to serve as the primary and continues to handle the requests from clients. Although the classic primary-backup replication is easy to understand and to implement, it can't acquire availability and consistency at the same time. If we need instaneous consistency between the primary and backup, the system will lose availability when certain failures occur. To keep the consistency, each transaction cannot be committed until the backup has received the log, which is referred as eager replication. However, if there exist faults at the network between the primary node and the backup or the backup has crashed for whatever reasons, it will lead to being unable to be the log successful replicated to the backup and the transaction unable to be committed so that the system is unavailable. On the other hand, lazy replication only requires that the primary asynchronously replicates the log to backup node, and the primary can commit a transaction without waiting for the backup to receive the log. In contrast with eager replication, lazy replication provides better performance but sacrifices the consistency in the case that the primary crashes but some committed log entries have not been transferred to the backup.

Log replication is the popular technique to achieve scalability and fault-tolerance in distributed systems. This interesting topic has long-term research history in database and distributed system communities. Especially in the distributed system community, the protocol family of Paxos-based replication has received more and more attention from both the academic and industry communities in recent years [3]. It is regarded as the only proven and best-practice solution for consistency and availability in distributed systems. In contrast with traditional primary-backup log synchronization, Paxos-based replication is able to eschew more complicate failure sequences when the dataset has 3 or more replicas [82].

Compared to the Paxos protocol, the recently proposed Raft protocol is relatively more easy to understand and has approximately 40 open source implementations. Leader election and log replication are the main procedures in Raft. Several machines constitute a Raft group, and each machine stays in one of three states, i.e., leader, follower or candidate. In the case of normal setting, there is only one leader and the other machines are followers. The clients send read/write requests or transactions to the leader. Then, the leader executes a transaction and replicates the log to the followers. After the majority of followers receive the log, the leader can commit the transaction and response to the client. During the log replication, the failure of minor followers will not make the system unavailable, and a few stragglers will have no effect on the response time. However, if the leader has became invalidated because of some reason such as network partition or system crash, some followers will transfer to candidates and initiate the leader election. The system continues to handle the request after the new leader is elected.

Although the protocols of Paxos family have been widely studied in the distributed system area, this is not enough research on how to effectively apply these consensus protocols to achieve the high availability of an OLTP system. Furthermore, the two objectives of high availability and strong consistency are in conflict. The consistency of the database state is guaranteed by the concurrency protocol, and there is a pressing need to study how the consensus protocol and concurrency control influence each other.

1.5 Organization

The rest of this book is organized as follows. In Chapter 2, we present an efficient multiple-version storage engine for in-memory data stores. In Chapter 3, we will introduce a scalable range optimistic concurrency control protocol for in-memory database systems, and this protocol is suitable for the hybrid workload with point access and key range scan operation. As modern database systems are designed and deployed on the cluster environment with commodity machines, Paxos-based log replication is widely used to provide the feature of high availability. In Chapter 4, we propose an efficient implementation of global snapshot isolation in in-memory database cluster. Then, we introduce a fast log replication scheme and recovery protocol in Chapters 5 and 6. Finally, we summarize the book in the last chapter.

2

Multi-version Storage Engine

2.1 Introduction

With the development of storage techniques, main memory has become the cost-efficient storage option for modern OLTP systems. The commodity servers equipped with a RAM of several hundreds Gigabytes have been widely deployed in the industry environment. The recently published systems, such as H-Store, Hekaton, HyPer, etc. have adopted the large memory as the main storage, and the disk is only used to store cold data. As the cost of conventional disk IO has disappeared and most OLTP transactions are executed in main memory, the highly efficient main memory storage engine increasingly plays an important role for in-memory OLTP systems.

Multi-version storage engine is the fundamental component of modern main memory data store using the popular multiple version concurrency control (MVCC). MVCC [75] has a property that read and write operations are never blocked by each other. Therefore, multi-version in-memory storage has been a common component of modern data stores [5, 57, 79]. The basic idea of MVCC is that the DBMS maintains multiple physical versions of each logical object to allow operations on the same object to proceed in parallel. Multi-version allows read-only transactions to access older versions of tuples without preventing read–write transactions from simultaneously generating newer versions. However, there is no one "standard" implementation of MVCC.

11

The straightforward implementation of the storage engine is to use a linked list to store multiple versions of an object. A read operation has to traverse the list for the specified version, which incurs pointer chasing. An optimization method implemented in HyPer is to store the current version in the object header, which is friendly to read the latest snapshot of data. However, a read operation still needs one extra jump in memory when accessing an object being updated.

There are several design choices that have different trade-offs and performance behaviors. Wu *et al.* have evaluated MVCC in a modern DBMS operating environment through experiments [99], where they also describe two kinds of schemes for the append-only version storage of MVCC. One is an *Oldest-to-Newest (O2N)*, where the lists HEAD is the oldest extant version of a tuple with the earliest commit timestamp (cts). But the DBMS potentially traverses a long version chain to find the latest version during query processing. The other one is an *Newest-to-Oldest (N2O)*, to store the newest version of the tuple as the version chains HEAD. Since most transactions access the latest version of a tuple, the DBMS does not have to traverse the chain. The downside, however, is that the chains HEAD changes whenever a tuple is modified.

To reduce pointer-chasing, some storage engines, like HyPer [71], embed the current (newest) version of an object in the object's header. Therefore, a read operation may get the current version in the object header, which avoids visiting the version list. However, when an object is being updated, the current version is pushed to the list. In other words, a read is required to visit the head of an N2O list when the object is being updated. This produces a memory jump, which can increase the response time of the query. Accordingly, the workload, whose reads operate on the dataset updated frequently, has a negative impact on the throughput.

In this chapter, we propose an efficient multi-version storage (EMS), a new storage scheme for a main memory data store. EMS embeds two newest versions in each object header and adopts an *O2N* version list, so that a read operation always gets the current version in the object header even as the objects are being updated. This may reduce the overhead of visiting the version list, which avoids some pointer-chasing operations. Then we present a snapshot isolation (SI) protocol using the new storage, which adopts lock-free mechanism. We implement a data store prototype based on our scheme, and the performance analysis demonstrates the effectiveness of our method in terms of read throughput.

This chapter is organized as follows. First, preliminary works which include SI and multi-version storage for main memory data stores are presented in Section 2.2. We introduce EMS and SI using our storage in Section 2.3. Section 2.4 describes the technique of checking point and recovery in the data store using EMS. Section 2.5 presents the performance evaluation. Related works are described in Section 2.6. We conclude the chapter in Section 2.7.

2.2 Preliminaries

In this section, we introduce the basic concept of SI and the traditional multi-version storage for main memory data store in SI. For ease of discussion, we assume that the system is a key value data storage.

2.2.1 Snapshot isolation

SI, which is one type of MVCC, was proposed by Berenson *et al.* [4]. In SI, each transaction reads data from a snapshot of the (committed) data as of the time the transaction started, called its start timestamp (sts). That is to say, whenever transaction i, which will be denoted as T_i, reads a data record x, it does not necessarily see the latest value of the record x. Instead T_i sees the version of x that was produced by the last committed one among the transactions updating x before T_i started. Read operations of a transaction under SI are never blocked.

The transactions writes (updates, inserts and deletes) will also be reflected in this snapshot, to be read again if the transaction accesses (i.e., reads or updates) the data a second time. Updates by other transactions that are active after the transaction's start timestamp are invisible to the transaction. When the transaction T_i is ready to commit, it gets a commit timestamp (cts), which is larger than any existing start timestamp or commit timestamp. The transaction successfully commits only if no other transaction T_j with a commit timestamp in T_i's execution interval $[T_i.sts, T_i.cts]$ wrote data that T_i also wrote. Otherwise, T_i will abort. This feature, called First-Committer-Wins (FCW), prevents lost updates. When T_i commits, its changes become visible to all transactions whose start timestamps are larger than T_i's commit timestamp.

2.2.2 Multi-version storage for main memory storage

The multi-version storage scheme specifies how the system stores multiple versions of a certain data object for concurrency control and what information each version contains. The data store uses the tuples pointer field to create a latch-free linked list called the version list. This version list allows the data store to locate the desired version of an object, which is visible to the read operations of a transaction. As we discuss below, the head node of a version list is either the newest or the oldest.

Pure O2N: As illustrated in Figure 2.1(a), the pure O2N storage adopts an O2N version list, which stores all the value versions of an object. The list's first node is the oldest extant version with the earliest commit timestamp (cts). The advantage of an O2N is that the data store does not need to update the pointer in the header whenever the object is modified. But the data store potentially traverses a long version chain to find the current object value. This is slow because of pointer-chasing, which may pollute CPU caches by reading needless versions. Thus, achieving good performance with an O2N is highly dependent on the system's ability to prune old versions.

Pure N2O: The other scheme is to adopt an N2O version list to store all the versions, which is shown in Figure 2.1(b). Since most transactions access the latest version of a tuple, the data store does not have to

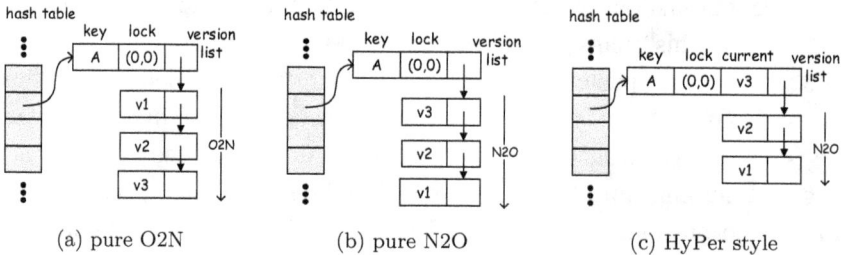

(a) pure O2N   (b) pure N2O   (c) HyPer style

Figure 2.1: (a) and (b) are regarded as general approaches to link multiple object versions from the oldest to the newest or vice versa and (c) demonstrates the multi-version storage format used in HyPer to improve read performance.

traverse the version chain. Like pure O2N, the object header only stores some metadata for the data object, e.g., the object's key and the lock information. However, the read thread, holding the object, also needs at least one jump in memory to get the current version. Also, the pure N2O storage is not friendly to an analysis task, which runs for a long time and may acquire the oldest version values.

HyPer style: The multi-version storage, like HyPer style, is an optimized scheme. As illustrated in Figure 2.1(c), the current version of an object is embedded in the object header and the version list is organized as an *N2O*. Therefore, when a transaction gets the newest snapshot, it may obtain the value in the header, which avoids the visit to the version list. However, the HyPer style storage has two weaknesses. First, an object being updated pushes its current version to the list. In other words, a transaction reading the object needs to visit the first node in the list. Second, due to the adoption of an N2O, a read operation obtaining the oldest snapshot has to traverse the version list.

2.3 Storage Engine

In this section, we will introduce a new EMS, which embeds two newest versions in the object header and adopts an *O2N* linked list. Then we present the implementation of SI protocol using the new storage engine. For ease of description, we assume the type of object value is inline.

2.3.1 Version storage

The design goal of EMS is to resolve two problems in the traditional storage engine. The first is to reduce the probability of point chasing resulting from reading the specified version from the linked list. The second is to avoid modifying the object head when generating a new version in an *N2O* linked list. In order to address these issues, we require a combination of advantages of an *N2O* and an *O2N*. And the lightweight lock mechanism and latch-free linked-list should be maintained. Therefore, we have to modify the object format for the new storage.

As illustrated in Figure 2.2, the object format for efficient multi-version store is similar to the traditional in-memory implementation, except there

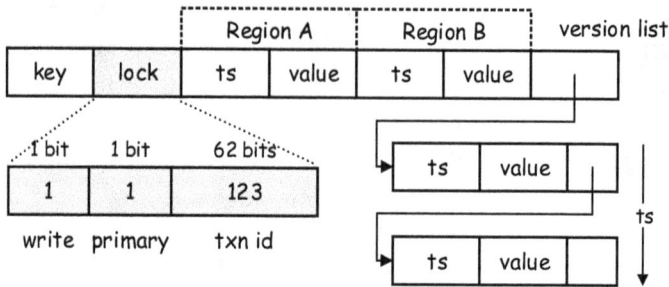

Figure 2.2: Object format for EMS.

are two value versions embedded in the object header. The ones labeled *region A* and *region B* are the two newest versions of the object. We use *primary* and *secondary* to denote the master version (i.e., the newest one) and the second newest version, respectively. The other old ones are linked in the *version list* — whose pointer is stored in the object header as well — in the order of their commit timestamps (cts). The lock field, a 64-bit word, consists of a *write-bit*, a *primary-bit* and 62 bits transaction id *tid*. The *write-bit* indicates whether the object is locked by a transaction write, and *primary-bit* represents that region in the object header which owns the master version. For ease of description, we use the *primary region* to denote the region indicated by the primary-bit. The other one is the *secondary region*. Let (*write-bit,primary-bit,tid*) denote the lock value of an object. For example, a lock value is initialized to (0,0,0), which shows that the corresponding object is not locked by any transaction and region A is the *primary region*. The value (1,1,123) in Figure 2.2 illustrates the object is locked by the transaction with *tid* 123 and region B is the primary region.

In order to facilitate the use of the lock, two interfaces are provided by the object as follows:

- acquire(*tid*): A transaction with *tid* acquires an object lock by using this interface of the object. It tries to set the lock value to (*1,p,tid*) by a compare-and-swap (CAS) instruction. Note that *p* is the original value of *primary-bit* in the lock word, e.g., its value is not modified by this interface. If successful, the lock value is changed and *true* is returned.

old	0	0	0		1	0	123		1	0	123

acquire (123)   release (false)   release (true)

new	1	0	123		0	1	0		0	0	0

(a) a txn with tid 123 acquires the lock   (b) release the lock when committed   (c) release the lock when aborted

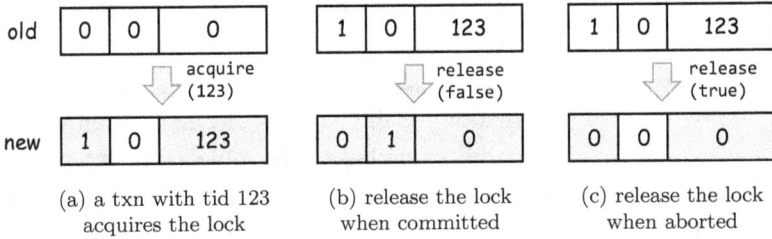

Figure 2.3: An example of lock operation.

- release($abort\_flag$) : The transaction releases a held lock by using this interface of the corresponding object. The parameter $abort\_flag$ indicates whether the transaction is aborted. If $abort\_flag$ is true, which means the transaction can be committed, the interface tries to change the lock value to $(0, \bar{p}, 0)$ by a CAS instruction; otherwise, the lock value is set to $(0, p, 0)$.

Figure 2.3 shows an example of lock value transformation by using these interfaces. The bits of lock l of an object, including write-bit and primary-bit, are initialized to 0. In Figure 2.3(a), a transaction t with tid 123 which needs to acquire a lock calls the object's function acquire(123). If successful, the lock bits will be set to the new value (1,0,123) and other transactions who want to acquire the lock will fail. If t can be committed, it will call the object's function release($true$). The lock bits are changed to (0,1,0), which is illustrated in Figure 2.3(b). If t is aborted, the release($false$) of the object will be called and the lock value is changed to (0,0,0). The result is shown in Figure 2.3(c).

Owing to 64-bit length of the lock, a word of common commercial server, all these functions can be implemented by a CAS instruction, which indicates that the lock is operated in the latch-free mode. In the following, we will combine the object format and the lock interfaces to introduce the transaction operations for SI.

2.3.2 Write operations

The data store supporting SI has to ensure that the concurrent transactions whose write sets intersect with each other are serializable. In our scheme, we adopt the two-phase locking (2PL) protocol to guarantee the serializability. In this subsection, we give a detailed description of the write operation using the new version storage.

When receiving a write request from a client, the data store first gets the transaction information for this session of client. Then it hashes the key of the requested object and gets the object header from the hash table. If the object does not exist in the memory table, the system will return an empty result to the client. Next, the transaction calls the write function, whose pseudocode is illustrated in Algorithm 2.1. The detailed execution flow of writing an object is as follows:

Algorithm 2.1: Write operation

---

1 Function write(*object, trans_id*)
   Data: A transaction with *trans_id* writes the *object*.
   Result: Whether the write succeeds.
   /* acquire the lock of *object* by a CAS operation */
2 if *object*.acquireLock(*trans_id*) then
3   *t* ← get the txn from txn manager according to *trans_id*;
4   *l* ← get the lock of *object*;
5   *pVersion* ← get the primary version of *object* using *l.pri*;
6   *sVersion* ← get the secondary version of *object* using *l.pri*;
7   if *t.sts* < *pVersion.cts* then
8   *object*.releaseLock(*true*);
9   abort the transaction *t*;
10   else if isValid(*sVersion*) *or* isExpired(*sVersion*) then
11   set *sVersion.cts* to *infinite*;
12   else
13   add *sVersion* to *object.version_list*;
14   set *sVersion.cts* to *infinite*;
15   end
16 end
17 end

---

(1) **Acquire lock.** Before modifying the object value, the transaction with *tid* should acquire its lock first. In other words, it calls the function acquire(*tid*), which tries to mark the lock. Recall that the acquire does not alter the *primary-bit*, which indicates that the position of the primary region remains unchanged. If the acquire returns true, the transaction will execute the next step; otherwise, the false is returned and the transaction needs to re-execute the write function.

(2) **Avoid lost update.** To prevent the lost update anomaly, the transaction needs to check the *cts* in the primary region. If the *cts* is greater than the *sts* of the transaction, the write operation will result in lost update. Therefore, the lock will be released by calling release(*true*) and the transaction will be aborted. Otherwise, we can proceed with the next step.

(3) **Handle secondary region.** Since the second region will be private to the transaction holding the object lock, it should be moved to the version list carefully. Therefore, the transaction needs to check the expiration and invalidation of the secondary version. More precisely, it first tests whether the *cts* of the secondary version is infinite. If yes, we claim that this version is invalid, and so the transaction can accordingly perform next step without any additional action; otherwise, it will examine whether there exists an active transaction whose start timestamp is in the range [*sec.cts*, *pri.cts*). If yes, it shows that this version has expired, the transaction will set the *cts* of the version to infinite directly; otherwise, it first adds the secondary to the version list, and then sets the *cts* in this region to infinite. Finally, the transaction can proceed to the next step.

(4) **Update value.** When the above steps are executed successfully, the secondary region is private to the transaction. Therefore, it can modify the value in the region safely. More specifically, it updates the value field of the private region with the input object value.

If the above steps are carried out, the transaction not only holds the target object lock but also updates the corresponding value. In reality, a transaction may modify a same object multiple times. Therefore, after it first updates the value successfully by the write function, the transaction only needs to perform step 4 when it updates the same object.

2.3.3 Read operations

Owing to the property of multi-version, a read operation in SI never needs any acquisition of object lock in our storage. Therefore, the process of read is different from the write execution described in Algorithm 2.1.

When the data store receives a read request for an object from a client, it tries to get the object from the memory table. If the target does not exist, an empty result will be returned directly; otherwise, it visits the object to get the expected value. The detailed execution flow of reading an object is as follows:

(1) **Check authority.** The transaction t gets the lock field of the object and checks its *write-bit* and *tid* bits. If the *write-bit* is 1 and the value of *tid* bits is equal to the transaction id, it shows that the object has been locked by the transaction itself. Since a transaction can read an uncommitted value written by itself, it accesses the secondary region directly and gets the corresponding value. Otherwise, it enters the next step.

(2) **Check primary and secondary.** According to the *primary-bit*, the transaction checks the primary region first. If the *pri.cts*, the commit timestamp in primary region, is valid and the transaction's start timestamp is $\geq$ the *pri.cts*, the *pri.value* will be returned. Otherwise, the transaction checks whether the secondary region is expected. If the transaction does not acquire the desired results, if proceeds with the next step.

(3) **Traverse version list.** If the read operation of the transaction does not get the desired values in region A and B, it will traverse the *O2N* version list. If the list does not contain any nodes, an empty result is returned; otherwise, the transaction can get the specified value in one version node.

2.3.4 The end of transaction

If the transaction executes all operations successfully, it will enter the commit phase, and a unique *cts* — a monotonically increasing

---

Algorithm 2.2: Read operation

---

1 <u>Function</u> read(*object, trans_id*)

    Data: Some input data

    these inputs can be displayed on several lines and one input can be wider than line's width.

    Result: Same for output data

2     $t \leftarrow$ get the txn from txn manager according to *trans_id*;

3     $l \leftarrow$ get the lock of *object*;

4     $pVersion \leftarrow$ get the primary version of *object* using *l.pri*;

5     $sVersion \leftarrow$ get the secondary version of *object* using *l.pri*;

6   if isValid(*pVersion*) *and t.sts $\geq$ pVersion.cts* then

7 | return *pVersion.value*;

8   else if isValid(*sVersion*) *and t.sts $\geq$ sVersion.cts* then

9 | return *sVersion.value*;

10   else if *object.version_list $\neq$ null* then

11 | $vNode \leftarrow$ get the first entry of *object.version_list*;

12 | while *vNode $\neq$ null* do

13 | | if *vNode.next $\neq$ null and vNode.next.cts > t.sts* then

14 | | | *vNode $\leftarrow$ vNode.next*;

15 | | else

16 | | | return *vNode.value*;

17 | | end

18 | end

19   else

20 | return *null*;

21   end

22 end

---

number — is allocated to the transaction; otherwise, it will be aborted. Note that an object lock should be released when the transaction holding the lock ends.

- If the transaction can be committed, it will release all the locks held by itself. More precisely, for each object in its write set, the transaction sets the *cts* of the secondary version first. And then it calls the function release(*false*). Recall that the function resets the *write-bit* and *tid* bits to 0, and relocates the primary region. Finally, it sets the global published timestamp to its *cts*, which will be the start timestamp for subsequent transactions.
- If aborted, the transaction should release the locks by calling the function release(*true*) of the objects which it locked before. Note that for each object in the write set of the transaction, the primary region is not changed and the secondary region does not need to be compensated.

2.3.5 Garbage collection

Garbage collection is a key component of multi-version data store. In normal processing, an object update operation of a transaction could create a new version for the specific object, which increases the size of memory table. Due to the limitation of capacity of main memory, the store system should collect the expired versions. In our multi-version storage, there is a garbage collection manager (GCM) which takes charge of freeing the memory. An expired version which is detected by a worker is added to the GCM first. And then the GCM frees the memory of these versions periodically. The three ways of detecting unused values are as follows:

- Recall from Section 2.3.2 that when a transaction writes an object, it checks the secondary region. If the version is expired, it will update the value of the region in-place, except that the value is not inline. In other words, if the value word stores a pointer of actual value, the transaction will put it to the GCM.
- When a transaction has to traverse the version list to get the expected value, it checks each node visited. If the version of a node is expired, the transaction adds the node to the GCM and deletes it from the list.

• There is a background thread which scans and checks the whole storage periodically. Specifically, the thread scans the objects in key order and checks the secondary version and the nodes in version list.

2.3.6 Correctness

When a transaction acquires the lock of the object, it gains the update right to the place of secondary version, which is visible to other transactions unless its commit timestamp is invalid (infinite).

We show the correctness of the SI protocol based on our multi-version storage. We prove that the read operation always gets the correct version value from the storage.

Recall from Section 2.3.3 that a transaction with start timestamp visits the versions of an object in the specified order. Specifically, it accesses the primary region, the secondary region and the version list in turn. There is no doubt that if an object is not updated during a transaction read, the read operation will get the correct version value of the object.

If an object is being updated during a transaction read, the read operation will obtain the correct object value as well. Note that the secondary version of the updating object is moved to the version list. Since the primary region is not modified, if the primary version conforms to the read, the transaction can get the corresponding value. Since the old values in the version list are not changed, if the values in the primary and secondary regions do not conform to the read, we must get the expected value in the version list. Recall that the write operation moves the secondary version to the version list first, and then updates the *cts* of the region.

2.3.7 Analysis

Jump number

We compare the memory jump of EMS and other storages. We ignore the number of jumps in memory while a read thread gets the object and only focus on the number of jumps for acquiring the expected version

Table 2.1: Comparison of access overhead in different multi-version storage schemes.

Access Version	Pure N2O	Pure O2N	HyPer style	EMS
Current version	*one*	*m*	*zero*	*zero*
Current version (updating)	*two*	*m*	*one*	*zero*
Oldest version	*m*	*one*	$m-1$	*one*
Oldest version (updating)	$m+1$	*one*	*m*	*one*

after the read thread obtains the object. Assume that there are m versions in an object. We pay attention to four different scenarios, i.e., a read gets the current version or oldest version of an object which is being updated or not. The results of the number of jumps is shown in Table 2.1.

Memory consumption

Since the object header embeds two value versions, the memory consumption of EMS may be larger than other schemes. However, the value field in the header only stores the memory address of the specified value. In other words, the header of EMS needs only two extra 64-bit words, which are relatively smaller than the size of the value itself. And when executing writes, the invalid version may be collected in EMS, which reduces the memory consumption. The corresponding experimental results are illustrated in Section 2.5.3.

2.4 Checkpoint and Recovery

In this section, we will describe the recovery of our MVCC storage engine. When the system restarts from a crash, it first uploads the latest checkpoint from local non-volatile storage. Then it replays the commit log from that checkpoint and installs the results from log entries in the order of log sequence.

Owing to the property of multi-version storage, it is easy for the data store to hold a snapshot at a physical point of consistency. A background thread, which is responsible for checkpoint, executes the persistence task periodically. In other words, it starts a read-only transaction and flushes the transaction's snapshot to disk. When the task is finished, the checkpoint is persisted successfully. Note that there is nothing about the checkpoint mechanism which is different from other in-memory data store, so we focus on the log replaying in the following contents.

For ease of design, we assume that a log entry contains the commit timestamp of the corresponding transaction and update operations in the log are idempotent. Before replaying, the log is read from the non-volatile storage first. In order to accelerate the log replaying, multiple threads are used to apply the committed writes. Each log entry, as a unit, is encapsulated a task that is pushed to the FIFO queue of a worker from a thread pool. Each work executes the tasks in local queue independently.

Applying writes in log replaying phase differs from the write execution in the normal processing in three respects: First, since the system does not process read requests in recovery phase, all updates of one object are only wrote to the fixed region (e.g., region A); second, a replay worker can modify an object only if it acquires the object's lock, and it releases the lock when this operation is finished; Third, because the *cts* of a write is known, the replay worker updates the value of the fixed region only if the *cts* of the region is infinite or less than the *cts* in the log entry the worker replays.

After the whole log is replayed, the snapshot at the time point when the system went down recovers for the storage. In order to guarantee the monotonicity of *sts* and *cts*, the *cts* of the last log entry is obtained and used as a start point for new transactions.

2.5 Performance Evaluation

In this section, we present the results of experiments that were run to compare the performance of our proposed version storage with other implementations.

2.5.1 Implementation

We implemented a prototype using our multi-version storage EMS in Java. To obtain the location of a specified object quickly, we adopt an array to organize data. Therefore, according to an object's key, we can get the array index for the object directly. There are a variable number of worker threads and a single commit thread, which are responsible for transaction execution and commit, respectively. To meet the workers' need, multiple producer threads, which can generate different workloads, are adopted. There are some other background threads in the system, like GC thread.

We compare the performance of our method with other comparison points, e.g., `pure N2O`, `pure O2N` and `HyPer style`, which were implemented in our prototype and described in Section 2.2.2.

2.5.2 Experimental setup

Now we describe the experimental setup and give a brief overview of the benchmark in this evaluation.

Platform setup: All experiments were run on a single machine, which is equipped with a 2-socket Intel Xeon E5-2620 v3@2.4GHz (a total of 12 physical cores), 64GB RAM and three-disk RAID 5 while running 64-bit CentOS version 6.5. The version of Java Virtual Machine (JVM) is 1.8.

Micro-benchmark: The benchmark operates on a collection of 2 million objects. We experiment with three different workloads, i.e., `write-only`, `read-only` and `read-updating`. `Write-only` updates objects with fixed-size value, e.g., 10 or 100 bytes. `Read-only` reads objects — which are not being updated — from the object collection. `Read-updating` reads objects locked by other write transactions. All read operations can specify the object version they wish to get, e.g., the current version and the oldest version.

2.5.3 Experimental results

We conclude four groups of experiments here. The first two groups measure the read performance for each of the competitors in different workloads, while the last two compare the memory consumption of `EMS` and `HyPer style`.

Throughput

We first measure the read performance for each multi-version storage. To differentiate the throughputs of querying current object versions and

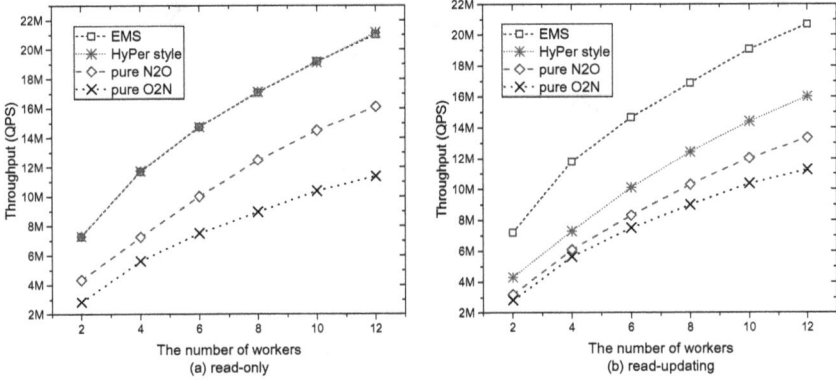

Figure 2.4: Comparison of throughput for accessing newest version.

querying oldest, we disabled the garbage collection and added three versions for each object before experiments. Due to the limitation of physical cores, the number of worker threads is restricted to 12.

Figure 2.4 shows the throughput of reading the current version. As the number of workers increases, we find that the throughput of each method is improved. Figure 2.4(a) shows the results in the workload read-only, and it can be seen that the performances of EMS and HyPer style are the same and are better than other schemes. This is because in the two storages, the current version of a object is stored in the header, which can help avoid the traversal of the version list. In the workload read-updating, whose results are illustrated in Figure 2.4(b), the performance of HyPer style is decreased since the current version of an object is pushed to the version list. Owing to the design of two versions in the object header, the performance of EMS is similar to the results in read-only.

When the oldest versions are accessed, Figure 2.5 shows the performance. Note that EMS and pure O2N have the same throughput results which are better than other schemes, because the oldest version of a object always exists in the first node of the version list. In the workload read-updating, the performances of HyPer style and pure N2O, compared to the results in read-only, are decreased. This is because a write transaction can put the current version to the version list, which increases the jump number in memory.

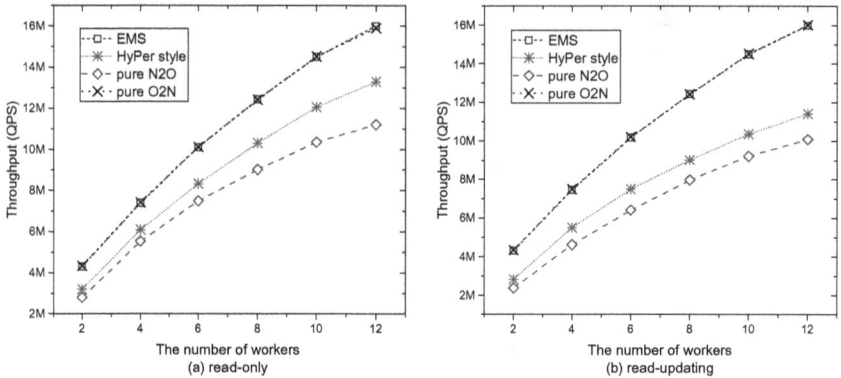

Figure 2.5: Comparison of throughput for accessing oldest version.

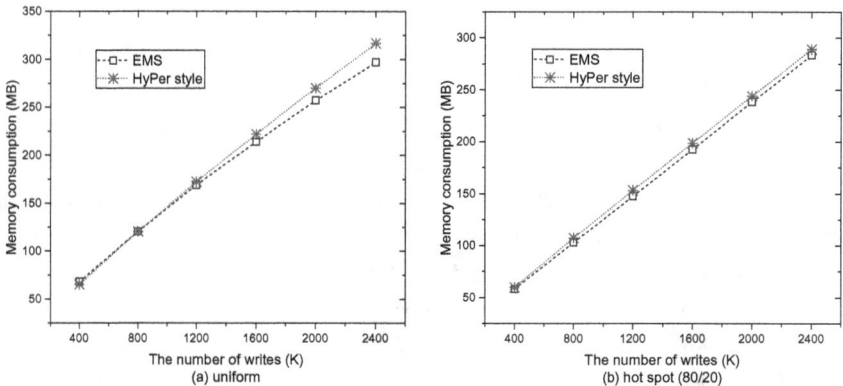

Figure 2.6: Comparison of memory consumption for updating 10-bytes value.

Memory consumption

We now pay attention to the memory consumption of our scheme. In order to evaluate the performance on memory consumption, we chose `Hyper-style` storage to be the comparison point. Figure 2.6 demonstrates that our scheme has a slight advantage over Hyper-style version storage as the write concurrency arises in a uniform random mode. When it comes to hotspot distribution which simulates $x\%$ of the operations access $y\%$ of the data items, we used a hot set comprising 20% of the database and a workload with 80% of the operations accessing the hot set. Then from the right part of Figure 2.6, we can

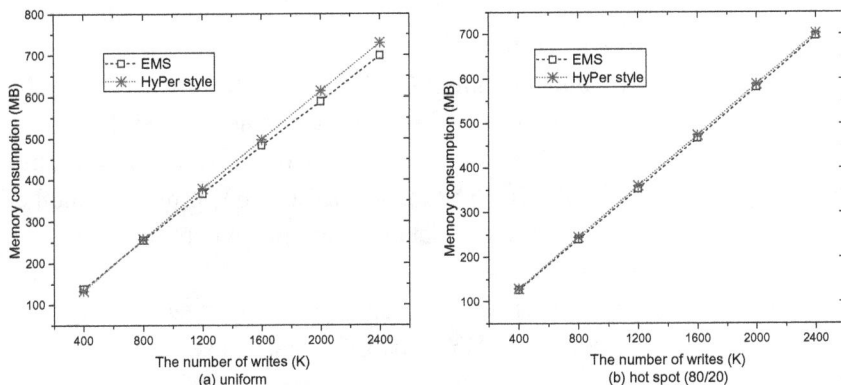

Figure 2.7: Comparison of memory consumption for updating 100-bytes value.

see that these two kinds of schemes consume nearly the same size of memory in a hotspot writing mode. It is also reasonable the memory consumption has a linear growth along with the increasing of writes number.

Meanwhile, the same comparison on updating 100-bytes value is also provided in Figure 2.7. The first group results shows that the memory consumption is not only related to the version scheme but also the size of data value. In a nutshell, the results and analyses above show that as far as memory consumption is concerned, our scheme performs slightly better than HyPer-style version storage. The main reason is that, although our scheme maintains one more version than HyPer-style, we do not have to push the secondary version into the version list when updating.

2.6 Related Work

An Experimental study of in-memory MVCC [75] detailed in Ref. [99] concludes information on version storage, garbage collection and index management. The authors summarized demonstrated as an O2N and an N2O. At the same time, they synthesized that the O2N has an obvious drawback since the DBMS potentially traverses a long version chain to find the latest version during query processing. However in an N2O, the chain's head changes whenever a tuple is modified, which may affect table's indexes at the same time.

Hekaton [24, 56] and PostgreSQL[a] [79] actually employ the O2N version storage. All the record versions are maintained at a single space. Besides, Hekaton is based on a timestamp-based optimistic concurrency control [53] variant of MVCC. The author of Ref. [63] proposed another MVCC scheme for main-memory database systems where the main idea is to use ranges of timestamps for a transaction.

There are more systems adopting an N2O version storage schema, such as MemSQL[b], NuoDB[c], HYRISE [32], etc. However, HyPer [71] moves forward with its version maintenance beyond an N2O where the latest version of each key is kept in-place, designed for guaranteeing serializability. It improved the performance of MVCC DBMSs with transaction-local storage optimization to reduce the synchronization cost. These schemes differ from the conventional append-only version storage scheme that suffers from higher memory allocation overhead in main-memory DBMSs. SAP HANA [57, 87] stores the oldest version in table space for garbage collection besides the version space that stores newly added versions in an N2O manner. All of these systems implement auxiliary structures based on an N2O schema for respective targets, still not avoiding the additional pointer skip, especially when the version is updating.

As for garbage collection, Silos epoch-based memory management approach allows a DBMS to scale to larger thread counts [93, 109]. This approach reclaims versions only after an epoch (and preceding epochs).

2.7 Conclusion

Multi-version in-memory data store is a popular choice for modern OLTP applications. The conventional implementations have some problems. In this chapter, we propose an EMS, a new storage engine for main memory data store. EMS embeds two latest versions in each object

---

[a]PostgreSQL. http://www.memsql.com, 2017.
[b]MemSQL. http://www.memsql.com, 2017.
[c]NuoDB. http://www.nuodb.com, 2017.

header, so that it can avoid the overhead of traversal of version list, especially in the update-intensive scenario. We present an implementation mechanism of the widely used SI level over EMS. The experimental results demonstrate that EMS outperforms the exiting multi-version storage engine of well-known main memory data stores in terms of throughput without excessive memory consumption.

3

Range Concurrency Control

3.1 Introduction

Modern in-memory database systems have been commonly deployed over multi-socket, multi-core servers with large memory. Machines with tens of CPU cores have been widely used in the industry, and the direction of processor development is towards increasing the number of cores [21,81]. However, it is hard to scale out the performance of transaction processing with the number of cores. The main reason is that conventional concurrency control mechanisms were designed at the era of database systems using disks as the primary storage medium and the deployment was generally equipped with a small number of processors [1,35,40,89,102]. The concurrency control aims to maximize the number of concurrently executed transactions and at the same time to guarantee the data integrity. The old approach traditionally hides the expensive disk IO cost through buffer management. However, the overhead of traditional disk IO and buffer management have disappeared in modern in-memory OLTP systems such that the concurrency control scheme itself has become the main bottleneck of high-performance transaction processing [45,84]. Compared with the well-known two-phase locking (2PL) protocol, the optimistic concurrency control (OCC) scheme and other similar variants allow transactions to execute concurrently in a lock-free manner and thus have been revisited and adapted for multi-core systems [24,27,49].

33

The serializability is the major criterion for correctness when scheduling concurrent transactions. OCC guarantees a schedule to be serializable by validating whether the read set of a transaction is modified by recently committed transactions. If a record in the read set has been updated by some other committed transactions, it means that this transaction has the risk of violating serializability because of the stale read and thus would be aborted. The primary overhead of OCC protocol is to determine the serial order of transactions, which is referred to as validation cost. Compared with the cost of executing transaction logic, validation cost is relatively small based on the assumption that the transaction only reads a small number of records.

The validation phase takes a significant effort to validate the key-range scan operation under heterogeneous workloads. Recently proposed OCC variants for in-memory database systems adopted two categories of methods to guarantee the correctness of range scan. The first approach requires transactions to keep the records within the scanned range in the read set [24,56,67,93]. At the validation phase, the version of each record in the read set will be verified to detect whether the record has been modified by other life cycle overlapped transactions. Therefore, this approach is referred to as Local Readset Validation (LRV). The drawback of this first strategy is the heavy validation cost when there are many records within the key-range. Silo adopted LRV and optimized it for phantom detection by checking the version change of B-Tree nodes which cover the scanned key-range [93]. However, it still needs to maintain all scanned records and re-read them for validation. The second validation strategy resolves this problem from another point of view. It assumes that OLTP workloads only contain a small number of write operations. To guarantee the schedule of transactions with range scan to be serializable, the transaction needs to access the write sets of previously committed transactions, and the validation succeeds if no records from these write sets belong to the protected key-range [53,71,83]. HyPer employs the selection predicate to represent key-range scan and detects the conflicts by validating whether the records in the write sets of other life cycle overlapped transactions satisfy the predicate, referred to as Global Writeset Validation (GWV) [49,71]. Compared with the first method, the second one only needs to access the relatively a small

Validation   Abort   Useful Work

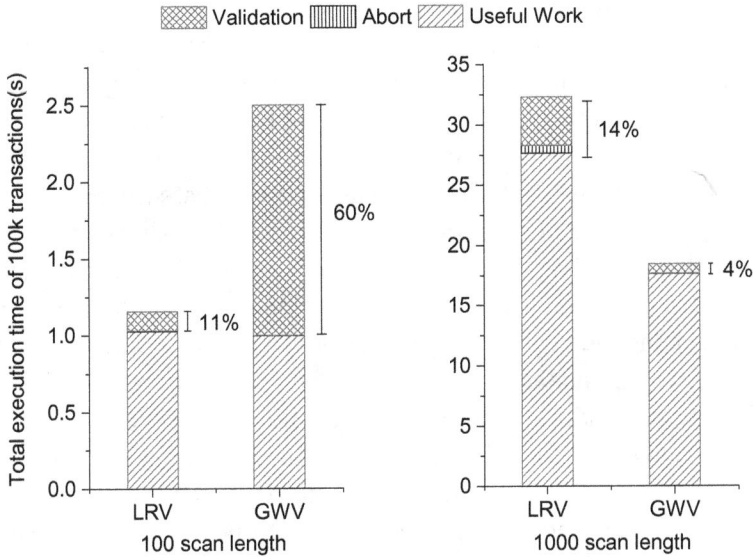

Figure 3.1: Exploration of the time-consuming part of transaction life cycle in OLTP-like (left) & OLAP-like (right) workloads. The OLTP workload has 10% transactions including key-range scan over 100 keys, and OLAP workload has 90% transactions with scan operation in a relatively large key-range cross 1000 keys.

number of written records under the read-intensive workloads. However, in the case of write-intensive workload, the gains of this method are reduced since the number of overlapping transactions to be checked significantly increases.

We have evaluated the above-mentioned two OCC protocols over OLTP-like and OLAP-like workloads by extending the YCSB benchmark [17], and the coarse-grain performance profile is presented in Figure 3.1. In the OLTP workload, each transaction contains five write operations and only 10% transactions contain a relatively short key-range scan over 100 keys. As we can see, LRV works better than GWV in the OLTP workload. The reason is that the read set only contains a small number of records in the OLTP workload. In this case, Silo just takes minimum cost to maintain the small read set and to validate each record in the short scanned range. However, since the OLTP workload is write-intensive, GWV needs to validate many writes from other overlapped transactions so that its validation cost overweighs the time of executing transaction logics, i.e., useful work. In the OLAP workload, the validation scheme of LRV is required to hold a large read set during the execution of transaction. In addition to maintaining the read set, checking each record version in this set exacerbates the cost of transaction execution. This leads to the result that LRV has worse performance compared to GWV.

In this chapter, we propose a scalable range-based optimistic concurrency control (ROCC) protocol to optimize the validation phase of transactions including key-range scan operations. The basic idea of Range-based Validation (RV) is that the global key space of records is partitioned into logical ranges and each range has a lock-free list to maintain which transactions have modified the records in this range. During the validation phase, the transaction will check the lists of its scanned ranges to find the modified records from other concurrent transactions and decide whether or not to abort this transaction. This approach has two advantages. First, ROCC does'nt need to find the overlapping transactions from a large number of recently committed transactions. To obtain all recently committed transactions, we usually need a highly centralized list which is not multi-core-friendly. Second, ROCC optimizes the validation phase to limit the conflict detection on part of the transactions which contain write operations in the scanned range, and then it can reduce the count of transactions to be validated.

3.2 Range Concurrency Control

Compared to serializing transactions which only contain operations at the record level, it is harder to provide the serialization isolation for the transactions with range scan operations. The locking-based pessimistic concurrency control resolves this problem by using a multiple granularity locking protocol to prevent the conflict writes or phantom records occurring at the specified range [31]. Although OCC has been regarded as a better choice for the situation of high-performance transaction processing, there is still a scalability problem under heterogeneous workload mixed with write and range scan operations. In this section, we first briefly review the original OCC protocol proposed by Kung and Robinson [53]. Then we present the overview of ROCC model with a motivating example.

3.2.1 Optimistic concurrency control

The OCC divides the transaction execution into three phases. We summarize these phases in the context of in-memory database systems where the whole dataset can be held in the large memory.

(1) **Read Phase.** A transaction optimistically executes its read or write operations without any blocking in this phase. The read and write sets are used to locally store the records that are read and written by itself, respectively. For read operations, the transaction first finds the record from the write set for the purpose of being able to read the uncommitted data generated by itself. If the write set doesn't contain this record, it needs to read the latest committed record from the in-memory table and save it into its read set. Obviously, dirty read anomaly is avoided in the OCC protocol.

(2) **Validate Phase.** OCC protocol determines whether or not to commit the transaction by detecting the serializability violation. Härder proposed two validation methods, i.e., backward and forward validation [34]. The backward validation is to validate the overlapping transactions which may be committed or may have completed the read phase. If there exist non-empty intersections between the read set of validating transaction and the write set of recently committed transactions, this means the later committed transaction has read the old data and thus violates the serializability. Forward validation requires the transaction to compare its write set with the read sets of currently executing transactions which stay at the read phase. In contrast with backward validation, forward validation has the flexibility to choose the validating transaction or active transaction to abort.

(3) **Write Phase.** If the transaction is successfully validated, its local write set can be applied and visible to other transactions.

The original OCC assumes that the actual conflicts are rare among concurrently executing transactions and most transactions are short. However, this assumption is broken in the case of heterogeneous workloads including small updates (OLTP) and short/long scans (OLAP). This kind of mixed workload often appears in the hybrid OLTP & OLAP database systems [27,49,78]. Since OCC needs to validate if a record in the read set is modified by other concurrent transactions, the validation cost grows along with the size of read set. In the scan-heavy workload, transactions take a significant effort to maintain the entire read set locally and to check the scanned records by re-reading them. The time-consuming validation on range scan operations may delay committing the transaction, and thus it further increases the probability of violating serializability validation, which will lead to high abort rate.

3.2.2   Range-based OCC overview

In this section, we introduce our ROCC algorithm, which uses the RV method. To clearly demonstrate ROCC, we give two motivating examples for GWV and RV, respectively, in Figure 3.2, and it shows how ROCC reduces the validation cost using logical ranges.

In GWV, the transaction first obtains a startTime-stamp from the counter before entering the read phase, and it obtains a commitTime-stamp from the same counter after completing its read phase [71]. Transactions are serialized according to the aligned commitTime-stamp by which they are sorted in a list. These two time-stamps are used to help find which transactions have been committed during the read phase of the validating transaction. As we can see from Figure 3.2(a), transactions from T_2 to T_5 are committed during the read phase of T_x. Under the commit protocol of GWV, T_x passes the validation only if there does not exist any committed writes from T_2 to T_5 which satisfy its read predicates. In this example, we assume that the key space is from a to z. Since the write set of T_5 is $W\{c, y\}$ and the record with key y satisfies the predicate of $key > u \wedge key < z$, the transaction T_x should be aborted.

As GWV only uses startTime-stamp and commitTime-stamp to find the transactions to detect the potential conflict, T_x needs to validate four transactions. However, there is only one transaction's write set that intersected with its scanned key-range.

In order to reduce the validation cost, GWV filters out the lifetime overlapped but *unrelated transactions* which do not intersect the validating transaction in the scanned ranges. First, the key space is partitioned into a set of logical and continuous key-ranges. Figure 3.2(b) presents a toy

Recent transactions

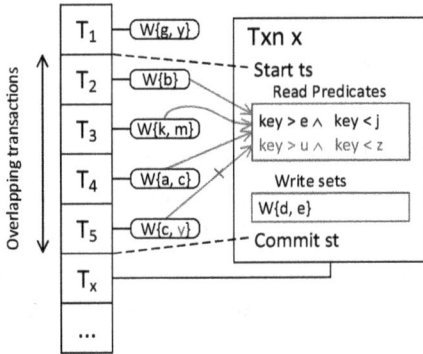

(a) Validation via a global txn list.

Recent transactions in logical ranges

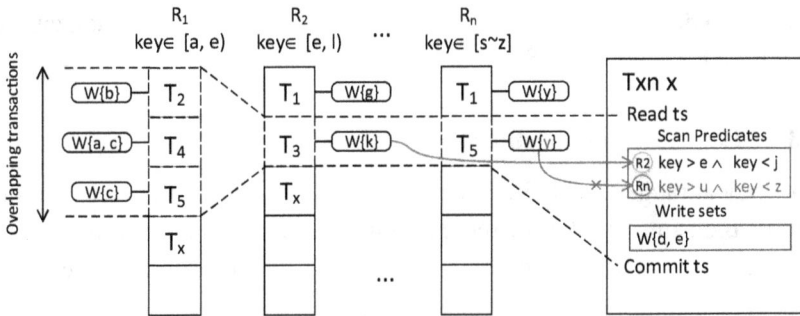

(b) Validation via txn lists in logical ranges.

Figure 3.2: Illustrating examples for comparing GWV (a) to RV (b). To validate no write violates scan queries, GWV maintains recent write transactions in a global list and RV maintains those in logical ranges.

range partition example where each range includes a set of keys. A list is attached to each range to keep the recently committed transactions which have write operations on this range. For instance, T_5 is inside the lists of R_1 and R_n because T_5 has written the records with keys c and y where c belongs to R_1 and y belongs to R_n. Second, we transform the read predicate of T_x into several logical key-ranges which cover the key space scanned by this predicate. In Figure 3.2(b), the predicate of T_x is transformed into two key-ranges which are R_2 and R_n, respectively.

Thanks to detecting conflicts at range level, RV finds only that write operations on R_2 or R_n may change T_x's reads. Instead of validating four transactions by GWV, RV just needs to validate two transactions for T_x.

3.3 ROCC Implementation

In this section, we introduce the implementation details of our ROCC model. In Section 3.3.1, we introduce the definition of the logical key-range and range structure which will be used to maintain recent transactions. Then in Section 3.3.2, we present how to maintain the predicates for the scan queries according to key-range definition. Section 3.3.3 explains our range-based concurrency control algorithm with commit protocol, and the phantom anomaly is analyzed in Section 3.3.4. We also mention the garbage collection and the reorganization for logical ranges in Sections 3.3.5 and 3.3.6, respectively. Finally, we prove the serializability of our ROCC model in Section 3.3.7.

3.3.1 Logical ranges definition

The logical ranges are defined over the key space, and each range contains almost the same number of records. Figure 3.3 shows an example where the index keys (from a to z) are partitioned into n logical ranges from

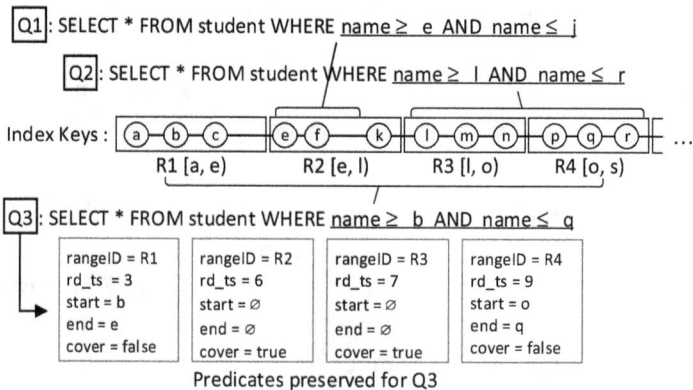

Figure 3.3: The key space is partitioned into logical key-ranges of equal size. The scan conditions of each query are mapped to several predicates. Each predicate corresponds to one logical range and records the detailed access information for later transaction validation.

R_1 to R_n. This key space is divided into small logical ranges which are continuous and disjoint from one another. Each logical range contains keys from the key range *start key, end key*.

ROCC creates a list for each logical range to maintain the pointer of transactions which has the have intention of modifying the corresponding logical range. These transactions in the list are sorted by their commitTimestamp order. When the transaction in this list is no longer needed, it will be removed periodically by garbage collection (see Section 3.3.5).

Initially, the key space is divided into specified logical ranges of roughly equal size. However, the number of records in each logical range may vary differently after the database has been running for a period of time. This may lead to performance hotspots in some logical range, and thus the key space needs to be re-divided periodically. We introduce the solution for range reorganization in Section 3.3.6.

3.3.2 Predicates for scan queries

A query may scan the records belonging to multiple logical ranges. ROCC maps its scan conditions to multiple predicates. Each predicate only corresponds to one logical range and has four variables $\{ID, ts, start, end\}$ to record when the query scans the exact scope of the logical key-range. The ID is the identifier of the logical range. The exact scope is recorded by *start* and *end*, where the key of *start* is included and the key of *end* is not included. *ts* denotes the timestamp at the beginning of scans.

Figure 3.3 shows examples of the predicate mappings for three scan queries. For query Q1, we maintain one predicate because the scanned records of Q1 are all inside the R_2. And two predicates for query Q2 which intends to access the data from R_3 and R_4. Q3 intends to access four logical ranges, thus we use four predicates.

3.3.3 Commit protocol

Commit Protocol of ROCC guarantees the serializability of transaction schedule. In order to detect read–write conflicts at range level, on the one hand, ROCC uses the mapped predicates for a scan query to remember the version of key-range scanned by this query. On the other hand, ROCC requires the transaction to register its the write operation in the corresponding logical key-range. The ROCC commit protocol is described in Algorithm 1. We prove the serializability guarantee of this protocol in Section 3.3.7.

Timestamp management

The life cycle of each transaction is defined by startTime-stamp and commitTime-stamp, where the startTime-stamp is the time of when the transaction begins and *the commitTime-stamp is the time of serialization point before entering into the validation phase.* If the transaction has a generated commitTime-stamp, it means this transaction is either committed or just in the validation phase. The commitTimes-stamp is also used to represent the version of record and logical key-range. The record version would be updated if some transaction modifying this record has been committed. For each logical key-range, ROCC adopts a transaction list to track the recently committed or being validated transactions which have write operations on this key-range. The latest version of a logical key-range is represented by the largest commitTime-stamp of a transaction in its transaction list.

Read phase

In the read phase, the read records returned for non-scan request(read on single record) are copied to transactions' read set R and the written records are copied to transactions' write set W. In ROCC, locked records are treated as dirty data. If the accessed records have been locked by other transactions, the transaction will be aborted immediately.

ROCC maintains predicates for scan requests in the predicate set P. Each scan request may read records from several consecutive logical ranges. To guarantee the consistency of scanning records over multiple logical key-ranges, ROCC constructs a predicate p for each key-range before scanning this key-range. The interleaving of constructing predicate and then scanning the key-range is equivalent to the procedure of adding a read lock on an object and then read it. However, the main goal of using predicate is for validation and not blocking the write operation from other overlapped transactions. At the time of constructing the predicate p, $p.ts$ is used to keep the current latest version of its corresponding key-range. *p.startkey* and *p.endkey*, representing the exact scope of this predicate, are set after the end of scanning the records in required key-range. Finally, this predicate *p* will be added into predicate set *P* which is saved in the transaction's local memory.

Instead of copying all scanned records into the read set, ROCC tracks the reads of a scan queries using predicates for each scanned logical key-range. Thus, ROCC reduces the time of maintaining the scanned records in two aspects. It avoids copying the scanned records and their versions into transactions' local memory on the one hand, and also saves the time of memory allocation on the other.

Validation phase

Before validating the transaction, ROCC adds locks on all the records from the write set in the key order. For each write, the transaction atomically registers itself to the transaction list of this logical key-range in line 3 in Algorithm 1. The registration will change the version of a logical key-range, which indicates the intent to modify the records in this range. Other concurrent transactions which have scanned this range can detect the read–write conflict by checking the transaction list of this range. After locking written records and transaction registering, the transaction generates the commitTime-stamp as the serialization point.

The validation at record level is similar to standard OCC protocol. From steps 6 to 10, ROCC checks whether the read record has been modified by other transactions by comparing with its local version, i.e., the commitTime-stamp recorded in the read set, the current version in the table. ROCC validates the range scan operation by verifying all predicates in the predicate set *P* from steps 11 to 20. For each predicate, ROCC retrieves the overlapping transactions from the transaction list of the logical key-range, where these transactions' commitTime-stamps are between the *p.ts* and the commitTime-stamp of the validating transaction. If any write from the overlapping transactions satisfies the key-range from *p.startkey* to *p.endkey*, the transaction will abort.

For example in Figure 3.2(b), transaction T_x has scanned some records from R_2 and R_n. T_x needs to validate if other transactions have modified their reads by the maintained predicates. First, we check the predicate in R_2, which is $p[R_2]$. We check if there are the overlapping transactions in

---

Algorithm 3.1: Commit Protocol(T)

Data: read set R, write set W, scan predicate set P

1   for *record* ∈ *sorted*(W) do
2 | lock(*record*);
3 | *range_list* = *range_manager*.find_range(record);
    | *range_list*.register(T);
4   end

5   generate(*commitTime-stamp*);

    /* Validation Phase   */
6   for *record* ∈ R do
7 | if *record.ts* ≠ *reread_ts*(*record*) *or*
    | *record is locked by others* then
8 | | abort();
9 | end
10   end

11   for *pred* ∈ P do
12 | *range_list* = *range_manager*.find_range(*pred*);
13 | for *overlap_txn in range_list* do
14 | | for *record* ∈ *overlap_txn.write_set* do
15 | | | if *record* ∧ *pred* ≠ ∅ then
16 | | | | abort();
17 | | | end
18 | | end
19 | end
20   end

    /* Write Phase   */
21   for *record* ∈ W do
22 | write(record);
23 | unlock(record);
24   end

R_2 according to the timestamp $p[R_2].ts$ and the commitTime-stamp of T_x. We get T_3, which has modified this range and is overlapped with T_x. The write $w(k)$ in the write set of T_3 doesn't belong to the exact scope of the predicate $p[R_2]$. For the next predicate $p[R_n]$, we find the overlapped transaction T_5 and its write $w(y)$ satisfies the predicate $p[R_n]$. Accordingly, T_x is in a read–write conflict with T_5, and T_x will be aborted.

Write phase

If all the validations pass, the transaction commits the writes with its commitTime-stamp and releases its write locks. Transactions do not release their resources whatever they commit or abort until these resources are no longer used in any logical range. Transaction resources are finally reused by asynchronous garbage collection.

3.3.4 Phantom

Typically, the insert operations will lead to phantom anomaly when handling scan queries in most OCC-based systems. The difficulty of phantom detection is that the read set cannot track the record that has not existed at the beginning of the scan query and will be inserted in the near future.

ROCC adopts a predicative validation to detect the modifications in the scanned range. The predicate-oriented approach for validation is equivalent to adding a long duration predicate lock [4, 83]. Thus, the phantom problem is avoided naturally in ROCC. The inserted or deleted records by other transactions are maintained inside their write set in the same way as the updates. If a transaction has scanned these records, according to our commit protocol, the inserts or deletes will be detected and the transaction will be aborted.

3.3.5 Garbage collection

Figure 3.2 indicates that each logical key-range is assigned a transaction list for conflict detection in the validation phase. After one transaction has been committed or aborted, its resources cannot be released immediately until there are no other transactions using that data anymore. If the startTime-stamp of the earliest running transaction is larger than the commitTime-stamp of a transaction in the list, the resource of this transaction can be released asynchronously by the garbage collection thread periodically.

3.3.6 Logical ranges reorganization

At the very start of our ROCC implementation, logical ranges are defined by dividing the key space according to data volume and its distribution. However, records that are inserted or deleted may be mainly accumulated in some logical key-ranges which would lead to high validation cost for the accessing transactions. Thus, we design a scheme for ROCC to re-divide or to reorganize the logical ranges. The range reorganization doesn't interrupt the active transaction execution during the period of transiting range concurrency control from the old logical key-range to the new one.

Note that the purpose of dividing logical key-ranges is to detect the conflict between scans and point updates from different transactions. The transactions that will run on the new divided logical ranges should be aware that there are old transactions still running on the old logical ranges. In other words, after the logical key ranges are divided, the new transactions should register their writes and validate the overlapping transactions in both the old and new logical key-ranges. We call them transition transactions which are running in transition period. After all the old transactions are committed or aborted, the validation of new transactions can only be done on the new logical key-ranges.

3.3.7 Serialization analysis

In this section, we prove that ROCC is guaranteed to generate the serializable transaction schedule.

Lemma 3.1. *A transaction T can be committed iff no updates, inserts or deletes which are committed by any other transactions are intersected with any* predicate *in predicate set of T.*

Proof. We suppose that a record x_v scanned by T_i has been modified by another transaction T_j who has generated commitTime-stamp before T_i. Thus, the serial order is $T_j \rightarrow T_i$, and there is a read–write conflict between T_i and T_j. In this situation, T_i should detect the conflict and abort. Assuming the information of this scan operation is maintained in p, it can be proved that T_i would validate T_j in the logical range identified by $p.ID$. If so, T_i would go through the writes of T_j and detect this conflict successfully.

According to the read protocol, the event of constructing the predicate p, denoted by $Construct(p)$, happens before the event of scanning the record x_v, denoted by $Scan(x_v)$. We represent this happen-before relation as $Construct(p) \prec Scan(x_v)$. Since this record has been scanned successfully in the read phase, $Scan(x_v)$ should happen before $lock(x_v)$ of T_j. Thus, the registration of T_j in logical range $p.ID$ happens between $Construct(p)$ and getting commit point of T_j. Therefore, $Construct(p) \prec Register(T_j) \prec commit(T_j)$. According to the validation phase protocol, the validation of p occurs after getting the commit point of T_i. Thus, $commit(T_i) \prec validate(p)$. Since $commit(T_j) \prec commit(T_i)$, it can be derived that $Construct(p) \prec Register(T_j) \prec validate(p)$. According to the commit protocol, T_i will validate T_j. Because T_j's write $w(x_v)$ satisfies p, T_i will be aborted.

According to the write phase protocol, the inserts, updates or deletes are kept in transaction's write set locally in the same way. The read–write conflict caused by inserts or deletes can be detected by the transactions which have scanned them.

Therefore, a transaction can be committed iff no updates, inserts or deletes which are committed by other transactions are intersected with any predicates of the transaction. □

Lemma 3.2. *A transaction T can be committed iff no updates, inserts or deletes which are committed by any other transactions are intersected with any read in read set of T.*

Proof. In read phase, ROCC keeps the last modified timestamp of the read records in the read set locally. In the validation phase, the commit protocol re-reads the records and compares the last modified timestamp with the local record. If the timestamp has changed, it indicates that some other transaction has modified this record. Therefore, the transaction will be aborted. Otherwise, there is no change in the read set of T. The transaction T can be committed iff no updates, inserts or deletes committed by other transactions are intersected with the read set of the transaction☐

Theorem 3.1. *Our ROCC protocol is equivalent to a serial history in commitTime-stamp order.*

Proof. According to Lemma 3.1, if a transaction T is committed, no data which is committed by any other transactions is intersected with any read predicates of T. Thus, this is equivalent to adding a long duration predicate read lock before read phase and releasing the lock after commitTime-stamp. According to Lemma 3.2, if a transaction T is committed, no data which is committed by any other transactions is intersected with any read set of T. Thus, this is equivalent to adding a long-duration read lock before read phase and releasing the lock after commitTime-stamp. For updates, we use exclusive write locks at commit time. Thus, our ROCC protocol is serial equivalent in commitTime-stamp order.   ☐

3.4 Range Validation Cost Analysis

It is obvious that the validation cost is related to the consumed CPU cycles for validating records or transactions. We measure the cost by the number of records or transactions to be validated. LRV validates the scanned records by re-reading them and checking their versions. Thus, the validation cost of a scan transaction is linearly proportional to the number of scanned records when using LRV. In contrast, GWV examines all of its concurrent transactions to avoid read–write conflicts in the validation phase. Therefore, for each scan transaction, the validation cost of GWV is mainly affected by the average number of concurrent transactions. To optimize the validation, RV uses logical ranges to reduce the number of transactions to be validated. There are three major factors influencing the performance of RV, as explained in the following section.

3.4.1 Factors influencing RV

The first factor is the average number of scanned logical ranges. It is determined by *partition size* (i.e., number of records in a logical range)

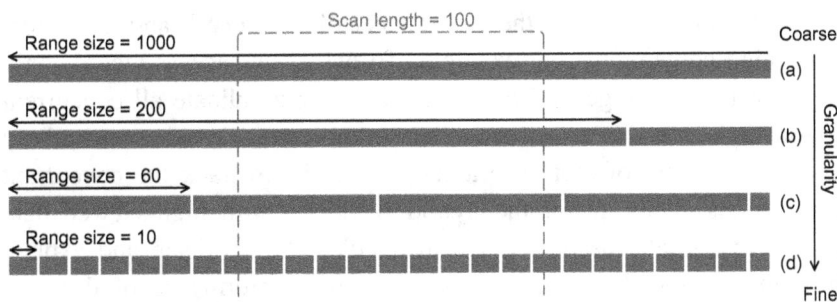

Figure 3.4: A scan example under various partitioning granularity.

and *scan length*. We illustrate how partition size affects the performance in Figure 3.4, which presents several cases of a scan operation covering a varied number of ranges. In Figure 3.4(a), it shows a coarse-grained partitioning where the range size is 10× larger than the scan length. The scan transaction needs to check all the transactions registered in its scanned logical ranges, though there might be only 10% transactions that perhaps have conflicts with it. Figure 3.4(d) shows the other extreme case of partitioning granularity, where the range size is 10× smaller than the scan length. However, this fine-grained partitioning cannot further improve the performance by filtering out more unrelated transactions. In this extreme case, smaller partition size in Figure 3.4(d) would only introduce more overhead of maintaining predicates and transaction registrations. Two kinds of reasonable partition sizes are presented in Figure 3.4(b) and (c), where the scan length is 0.5×–2× of the range size. We empirically demonstrate the effectiveness of the partitioning method in the experiment detailed in Section 3.5.6.

The second factor is the *skewness* of a workload. Since the contention is low in a non-skew workload, the accesses of a transaction are mostly not intersected with others. In this case, it is efficient for ROCC to filter out a large number of non-conflict transactions. In a high-skew workload, since a small amount of logical ranges receive most of the update requests, ROCC needs to validate a large number of transactions registered to these hot ranges. Therefore, the benefit of partitioning logical ranges will decrease.

It should be noted that the performance of LRV, GWV and RV suffers from high contentions. For example, if transactions access records only in a hot logical range, RV needs to register and validate all concurrent transactions in a single transaction list. In this case, RV behaves similarly to GWV as both of them use a centralized list to track the concurrent transactions. Thus, under the hybrid workload with high-skewed data access, RV is at least not worse than GWV. We evaluate and explain how the workload skewness impacts on the performance of different validation schemes in the experiment given in Section 3.5.5.

The third factor is the size of the circular array. To ensure that no updates violate the scanned predicates, RV needs to maintain the pointer of concurrent transactions by the corresponding circular arrays. If using a small size of the circular array, highly concurrent transactions may be blocked because of no available slots for transaction registrations, especially in the high-skew workload. The problem is alleviated by allocating a large size of the circular array, but it consumes large memory space. As a result, there is a trade-off between memory usage and performance. In our experiment, we allocate 5000 slots for each array and avoid transactions being blocked at the time of registration. Each circular array needs 40KB memory space. The key space is divided into 16384 logical ranges for the YCSB workload, and the total space used by the circular array is at most 600MB.

3.5 Experiments

3.5.1 Experimental setup

In this section, we present the evaluation of the ROCC protocol implemented in the DB×1000 codebase. DB×1000 is an in-memory DBMS prototype[a] which provides a pluggable framework to integrate different concurrency control protocols for performance comparison [103]. Existing integrated protocols include Silo, HEKATON, 2PL, etc. We compare the validation scheme of ROCC with those used by Silo and Hyper. In order to validate the key-range, Silo adopts LRV mechanism and needs to re-read the scanned range. Hyper uses GWV method for

---

[a]In *DBx1000*. https://github.com/yxymit/DBx1000.

Table 3.1: Details of experimental environment.

OS	CentOS 7
CPUs	2-socket Intel(R) Xeon(R) E5-2630 v4 Clockspeed 2.2GHz; Turbospeed 3.1GHz 20 physical cores; 40 logical cores (threads) 25M L3 cache
Memory	12*16GB DDR4 2400 MHz

checking the write sets from all other concurrent transactions. We set up the experiments on the machine described in Table 3.1. The single machine equipped with 192GB DRAM has 20 physical cores, and each one hosts two hardware threads.

3.5.2 Workloads

YCSB: The workload E of YCSB benchmark contains read, write and scan operations. The degree of workload skew is tuned by changing the parameter (θ) of Zipfian distribution. The read and write keys are selected according to the predefined Zipfian distribution. For scan operations, the start key of a scanned range is also selected by the same Zipfian distribution. We create two types of transactions to generate the hybrid workload by configuring the YCSB workload generator. The first one is a simple transaction which consists of five read/write operations, and each operation accesses a single record. The second is a bulk processing transaction containing four read/write operations and one key-range scan operation with a fixed length. The hybrid workload is a mixture of 90% simple transactions and 10% bulk process transactions. We generate the following four kinds of workloads with different Zipfian distributions which are the characteristic of workload skew:

- No-skew: Uniform distribution.
- Low-skew: A Zipfian distribution where $\theta = 0.7$.
- Medium-skew: A Zipfian distribution where $\theta = 0.88$.
- High-skew: A Zipfian distribution where $\theta = 1.04$.

By default, the access pattern of operations is low-skew. The data in the YCSB table is initialized to contain 10 million records. The YCSB table is partitioned into 16384 equal-sized logical ranges, where each one covers 610 records. A logical range is associated with a lock-free circular list. For each experiment, we run 100k transactions five times and measure the average throughput, latency and abort rate.

Modified TPC-C: TPC-C is a standard online transaction processing (OLTP) benchmark of mixed read-only and update-intensive transactions with a non-uniform data distribution. We modify the TPC-C benchmark according to the actual application requirement. In the recent online sales market, there is a growing demand for processing bulk scan operations in its workload. For instance, to promote consumption in the China Single's Day, the online shops often launch shoppers rewards program to reward the top shopper who has purchased the most in a certain period of time. According to the schema of TPC-C, we create a new bulk transaction that executes a scan operation in the customer table to figure out the top shopper in a randomly selected district who made the highest total payment from a certain start time, and this customer would be given the reward money to his balance. Thus, the bulk processing transaction of the modified TPC-C consists of one scan operation that randomly accesses a range in the customer table, and three updates on the customer, district and warehouse tables, respectively.

In the experiment, the number of processing threads is equal to the number of TPC-C warehouses. The original TPC-C transactions access its local warehouse and other warehouses with the probability of 85% and 15%, respectively. All bulk processing transactions only scan the local warehouse. Therefore, the bulk transaction has conflicts with the cross-warehouse Payment transactions. The hybrid workload is a mixture of 40% Payment transactions, 40% New-Order transactions, 10% bulk processing transactions, 4% OrderStatus, 4% Delivery and 2% StockLevel transactions. With 40 warehouses, the customer table is partitioned into 2000 logical ranges with equal size where a range contains 600 records.

3.5.3 Scan performance

In this experiment, we start 40 processing threads (bound to 40 CPU cores) and run YCSB and modified TPC-C workloads to evaluate the performance of three key-range validation schemes under hybrid workloads.

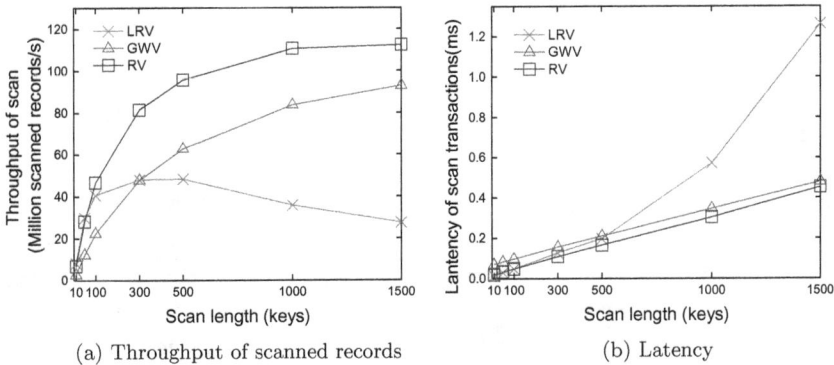

(a) Throughput of scanned records   (b) Latency

Figure 3.5: Results of the hybrid YCSB.

We combine 90% simple transactions and 10% bulk scan transactions, where the scan length varies from 10 to 1500 keys for hybrid YCSB workload and from 100 to 3000 keys for the modified TPC-C workload.

Figure 3.5(a) presents the overall throughput of scan transactions and Figure 3.5(b) shows the average latency of scan transactions. In Figure 3.5(a), as the scan length increases, the performance of LRV, GWV and RV reflects a growing trend proportional to scan length at the beginning. However, LRV's performance appears to decrease while the scanned key-range covers more than 300 keys. In the workload with the longest scan length (1500 keys), the performance of RV is about 3 times more than LRV and about 22% better than GWV. The overall trend demonstrates that RV can adapt to different scan lengths and achieve the best scan performance. From Figure 3.5(b), it is observed that LRV suffers from a sharp increase in the latency of scan transactions when the scan length is varied from 500 keys to 1500 keys. On the other hand, the latency of RV and GWV increases only slightly and the latency of RV is always lower than GWV.

The result of modified TPC-C workload is presented in Figure 3.6. Figure 3.6(a) and (b) show the performance and latency of scan transactions, respectively. It is observed that the three validation schemes demonstrate similar results to that of hybrid YCSB workload.

Result Analysis: The LRV strategy maintains all the scanned records in transaction local memory and re-reads them for validation,

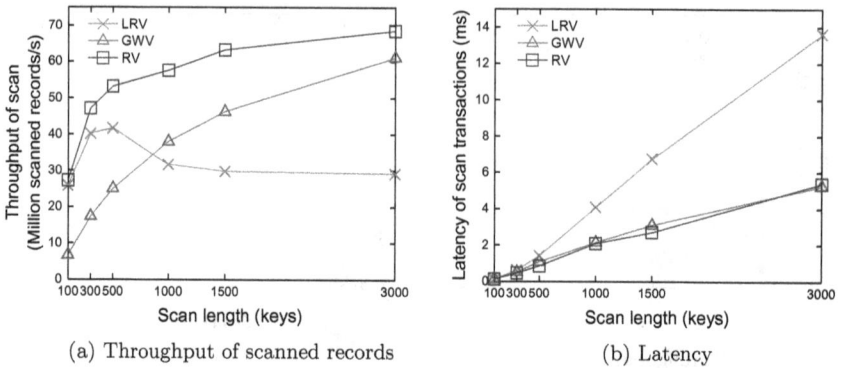

(a) Throughput of scanned records   (b) Latency

Figure 3.6: Results of the modified TPC-C workload.

which doubles the execution time before committing the transaction. Accordingly, the validation cost of LRV is mainly affected by the number of keys of the scanned range. It can be seen from Figures 3.5(b) and 3.6(b) that the latency of LRV increases at a higher rate with a larger scan range. Therefore, it is inefficient for LRV in the case of transactions containing large-range scan (e.g., 1500 keys). In contrast, both GWV and RV strategies validate the overlapping transactions that have modified its scanned logical ranges. Their validation costs are determined by the number of concurrent transactions. Under short-range scan workload (e.g., 100 keys), most transactions would be executed and committed in a relatively short time. In this situation, GWV takes too much effort on validating a large amount of recently committed transactions and thus leads to the low performance. Compared to GWV, instead of validating all the concurrent transactions, RV only validates a small amount of transactions having writes in scanned logical ranges. In other words, RV uses logical ranges to filter out unrelated transactions in the validation phase, which reduces the number of overlapping transactions to be validated. In addition, RV directly validates the key-range at range level if the scanned range is fully covered by the predicate. It can be seen that, compared to GWV, RV scheme significantly enhances the throughput under short-range scan workloads and is also efficient for large-range scan workloads. Compared to LRV, the main overhead of both RV and GWV is to track transactions by a list attached to

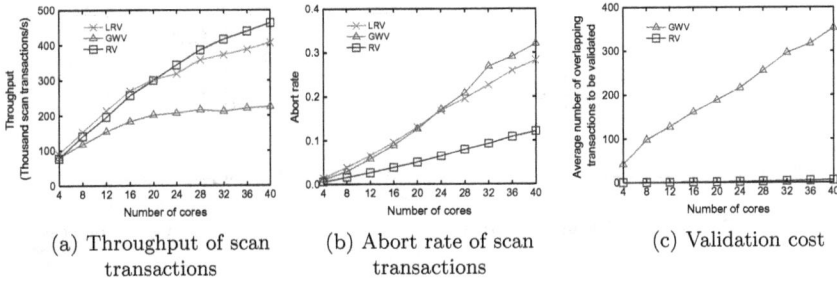

(a) Throughput of scan transactions

(b) Abort rate of scan transactions

(c) Validation cost

Figure 3.7: Results of YCSB workload with increasing cores from 4 to 40. The scan length is over 100 keys.

each logical range or by a global list, respectively. Because of this, it can be observed that the performance of RV is 10% worse than LRV under the very short-range scan workload (e.g., 10 keys). However, under large-range scan workloads, this registration overhead becomes insignificant compared to the gain from accelerating the validation. We make detailed overhead analysis for RV in Section 3.5.8.

3.5.4 Scalability

In this section, we evaluate the scalability of three validation schemes under YCSB and modified TPC-C workloads. The number of threads is varied from 4 to 40, and each thread runs the workload on an individual CPU core. The length of range scan for the YCSB workload is fixed to 100 keys, and it is about 3000 keys for the modified TPC-C workload. The experimental results of YCSB and modified TPC-C are presented in Figures 3.7 and 3.8, respectively.

Using more concurrent threads to run the workload can cause more data access collisions. Thus, it introduces transaction conflicts for scan transactions and leads to more aborts. As can be seen from the performance of YCSB workload shown in Figure 3.7(a), LRV is better with less than 20 threads but the rising trend of the performance becomes slow with more than 24 threads. RV method achieves near-linear scalability and the performance is the best with 40 threads. GWV is always worse than RV and LRV. With 40 threads, the performance of RV is 53% higher than GWV and 18% higher than LRV.

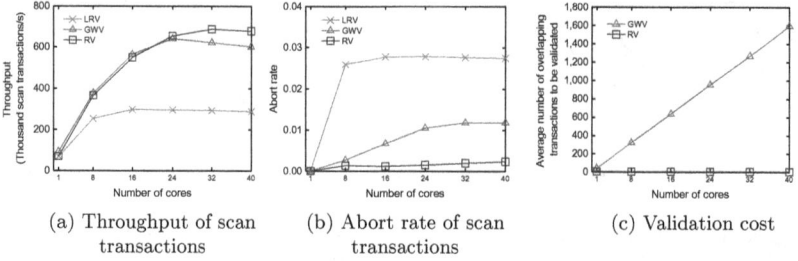

(a) Throughput of scan
transactions

(b) Abort rate of scan
transactions

(c) Validation cost

Figure 3.8: Results of the modified TPC-C workload with increasing cores from 1 to 40. The scan length is over 3000 keys.

The modified TPC-C workload is configured to scan a large range which contains 3000 customers. Under the setting of 3000 scan keys, the performance in Figure 3.8(a) reflects that LRV is poorly scaled up and almost stops growing by the 8 threads. RV achieves the optimal performance at the 32 threads and then declines slightly. GWV has the ascending curve of performance similar to RV, but starts to decline at 24 threads.

Result Analysis: We analyze the results by checking the average abort rate of scan transactions and the average number of overlapping transactions to be validated by GWV and RV. The average number of overlapping transactions determines the validation cost of RV and GWV. For LRV, it re-reads all the scanned records in the validation phase which consumes almost the same CPU cycles for scanning them. Thus, the validation cost of LRV is proportional to the length of the scanned keys.

Under the YCSB workload, LRV is required to validate 100 scanned records before committing a transaction. In the contrast, RV only needs to validate a few overlapping transactions containing writes. The number of writes is much less than that of scanned records validated by LRV. GWV needs to validate more than 300 writes from all the overlapping transactions, and Figure 3.7(c) demonstrates that its validation cost is for more than that for RV. In the modified TPC-C workload, the scalability of LRV is poor for its huge cost of maintaining a large amount of scanned records and validating them. This has further led to a rise in abort rate for LRV in both workloads, which is shown in Figures 3.7(b) and 3.8(b).

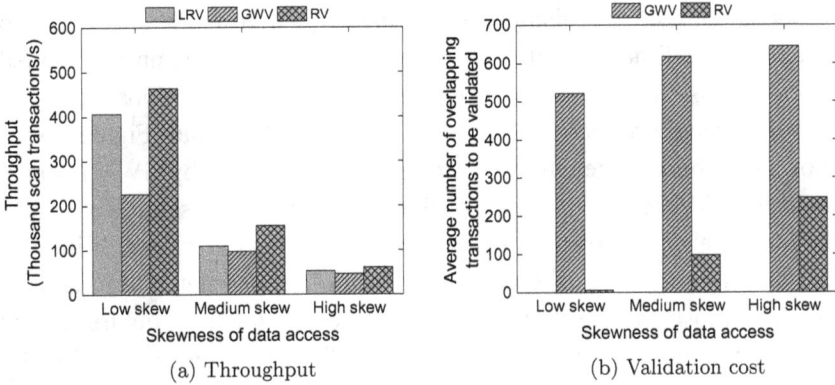

(a) Throughput

(b) Validation cost

Figure 3.9: Throughput of scan under skew workload.

The validation cost of GWV depends on the count of recently committed transactions. Under the multi-core setting, GWV would take more time in the validation phase because of more concurrent transactions. In the YCSB workload, although the writes of concurrent transactions will register to 16k logical ranges, transactions in only 5 logical ranges need to be validated (where the 3000 scanned keys cover 5 logical ranges at the most and each range contains 610 records). In Figures 3.7(c) and 3.8(c), it can be seen that GWV validates a large amount of concurrent transactions and RV only validates a very small amount of them. In addition, GWV uses a centralized list to maintain committed transactions which are likely to become a bottleneck in the environment of multi-cores.

3.5.5 Impact of skew workloads

We start with 40 threads to execute three skew workloads and make a comparison of the three validation strategies. The scan length is over 100 keys in the three workloads. The experimental results are presented in Figure 3.9. As is shown in Figure 3.9(a), RV achieves the best performance for the low-skew workload. Under the medium-skew workload, RV only performs slightly better. The three validation schemes have comparable performance when the workload is high-skew. The skew workload causes high contention and thus leads to more abort for scan transactions. In the low-skew workload, each logical range has relatively balanced transaction registrations. For the RV, a transaction only needs to validate a small number of transactions containing writes on its scanned ranges. Thus, RV is more efficient in the low-skew workload because most unrelated transactions can be effectively filtered out. Figure 3.9(b) shows that the average number of transactions validated by GWV is much more than RV. However, under medium-skew and high-skew workloads, the update and scan operations fall into several logical ranges. It implies that partitioning ranges cannot help filter out unrelated transactions because most of the transactions are really related. Figure 3.9(b) indicates that the validation cost of RV increases proportionally with the degree of skewness but is still lower than the validation cost of GWV.

3.5.6 Partitioning granularity

In this section, we evaluate the scan performance of RV under different partitioning granularity and various workload skew. The total number of keys is fixed to 10 million, and Table 3.2 gives five typical configurations of the number of logical ranges and the size of the logical range. The results are presented in Figure 3.10. Figure 3.10(a) shows how the scan performance varies with the number of partitioned logical ranges. The shaded area indicates a reasonable partition size for the workload according to the analysis given previously in Section 3.4. It is observed that the scan performance gets better with the increasing number of ranges from 1 to 16384 for all workloads with different scan lengths. The reason is that the proper partitioning granularity can effectively filter out the unrelated concurrent transactions and then reduce the validation cost. When the number of logical ranges exceeds 16384, for the workloads with the scan length over 100 and 300 keys, the performance has a stable trend. For the workload scanning 1000 keys, the performance drops nearly 30%. This result demonstrates that more

Table 3.2: Partitioning granularity.

Range count	1	16	4096	16384	262144
range size	10^7	6×10^5	2.4×10^3	610	38

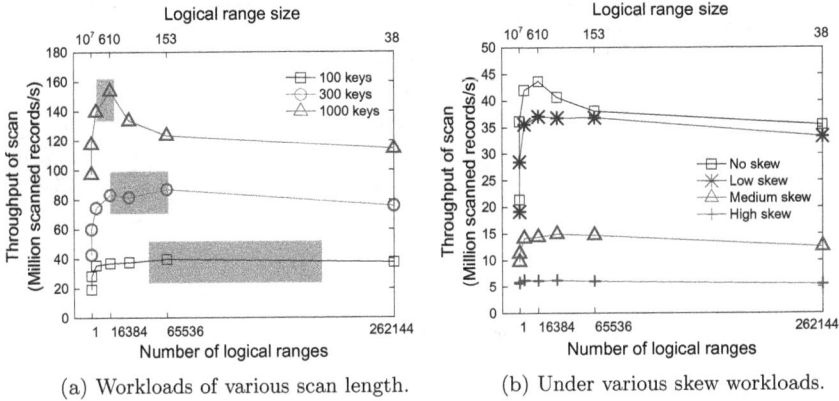

(a) Workloads of various scan length.   (b) Under various skew workloads.

Figure 3.10: Scan throughput with various partitioning granularity.

fine-grained partitions are not useful for long scan query. The reason is that when the scan length is much longer than the partition size, smaller partitioning granularity cannot make further reduction on the validation cost but introduce much overhead on maintaining more predicates for scanned ranges. The empirical result shows that RV achieves the best performance when the scanned key-range covers 0.5–3 logical ranges.

We also evaluate the performance of various partitioning granularities under different workload skew (with the fixed scan length over 100 keys), and the result is presented in Figure 3.10(b). It is observed that the more skew workload causes the lower scan throughput. We also find that the performance of non-high skew workloads continues to improve by increasing the number of ranges at the beginning, and when the number exceeds 16384 the performance begins to decrease. For the high-skew workload, as most of the data accesses focus on a few records, coarse-grained or fine-grained partitions really do not matter.

3.5.7 Circular array

In this section, we evaluate how the size of circular array affects the scan performance. We start 40 threads and run hybrid YCSB workload with fixed scan length over 100 keys. We change the array size from 100 to

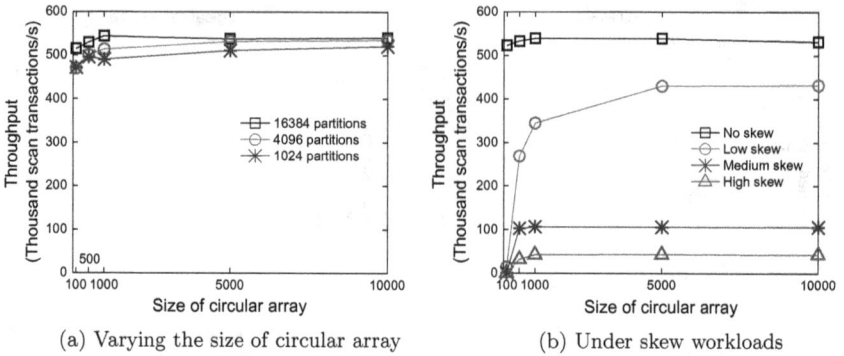

(a) Varying the size of circular array   (b) Under skew workloads

Figure 3.11: Scan throughput under various sizes of circular array.

10000 and evaluate the performance under various partition granularities and different workload skews. The results are presented in Figure 3.11. As we can see from Figure 3.11(a), the size of the circular array has a very small impact on the performance under different partition granularities. In Figure 3.11(b), we find that the small size of circular array has a negative influence on the performance under the skew workloads. It is always better to allocate a large circular array, but it may consume more memory. Tuning the array size is a trade-off between memory consumption and performance. We empirically allocate 5000 slots for each array. Under the setting of 16384 partitions, it approximately takes 600MB memory space.

3.5.8 Overhead analysis

The main overhead of ROCC is caused by registering update transactions to the corresponding list if they have writes in a logical range. In each logical range, ROCC maintains recently committed transactions in an optimized list implementation using a lock-free circular array. The circular array is operated by atomic instructions to reduce the extra cost consumed on registering transactions. However, it still leads to performance overhead in a write-intensive workload which has no bulk process transactions.

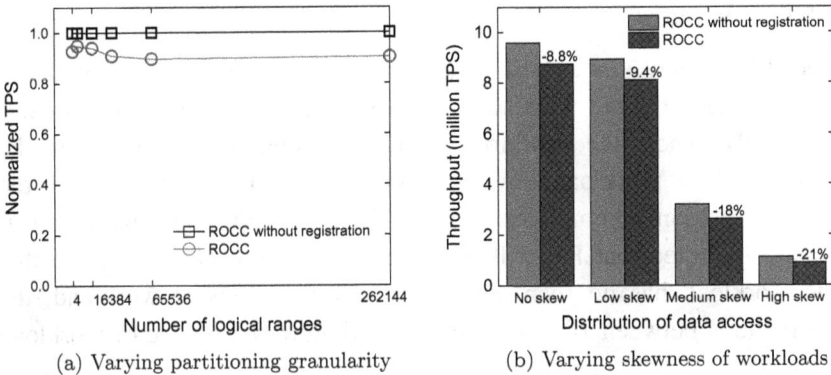

(a) Varying partitioning granularity

(b) Varying skewness of workloads

Figure 3.12: Performance under non-scan workloads.

We use the YCSB workload A to evaluate the overhead of transaction registrations, and the ratio of read to write operations performed in the YCSB workload A is 50/50. Each transaction is configured to consist of five operations without any scan queries. We turn off the transaction registration, referred to as ROCC without registration, and start 40 threads to run the workload. The experimental results are presented in Figures 3.12(a) and (b).

Figure 3.12(a) shows the comparison with various partitioning granularity settings. The TPS is normalized according to that of ROCC without registration. Since transactions register to the same logical range only once, it would make many registrations in the setting of fine-grained partition. It can be seen that the cost of the registration increases when using more fine-grained logical ranges. In spite of this, the overall overhead is less than 10%.

Figure 3.12(b) presents the performance comparison under different workload skew. The decline of TPS in no-skew and low-skew workloads is less than 10%. The overhead increases to between 18% and 21% in medium-skew and high-skew workloads. In the high-skew workload, it introduces the relatively high overhead caused by so many transactions competing for registering to a few logical ranges.

3.5.9 Summary

The RV achieves the best scan performance and scalability under a low- skew hybrid workload. Its advantage becomes more obvious especially when the workload contains larger range scan. In the medium-skew workload, RV performs slightly better and all of the three validation schemes are comparable in the high-skew workload. It should be noted that RV will introduce extra overhead in the case that the workload has no scan queries. In a write-intensive workload, the overhead is between 10% and 20% according to the degree of workload skewness.

3.6 Discussion

Deuteronomy introduced a multi-version timestamp ordering concurrency control for logical ranges (MVRCC) [59]. To avoid the phantom problem, the read timestamp of a key-range scan is required to be earlier than that of all uncommitted writes in the scanned ranges. Similar to MVRCC, RV also registers update transactions to the corresponding lists of logical ranges.

However, RV has two advantages over MVRCC. First, MVRCC needs to check more transactions than RV does for detecting read–write conflicts in logical ranges. MVRCC adopts a timestamp ordering concurrency control under which transactions are committed in the order of their start timestamps. While updating records in a logical range, transactions register to the transaction list of this range. These transactions are not ordered by their start timestamps in the associated list of a logical range. Thus, before executing a scan over a logical range, the transaction needs to examine the entire list to detect conflicts. In comparison, for each scanned range, RV maintains the start timestamp at the beginning of a scan operation and the validating timestamp at the validation phase. Therefore, RV only validates the overlapping transactions between the two timestamps instead of all the transactions in the entire list. The second advantage is that the conflict detection of RV is more precise than MVRCC for the boundary of scanned ranges. A scan operation may cover several logical ranges, and the boundary ranges (e.g., the first or/and the

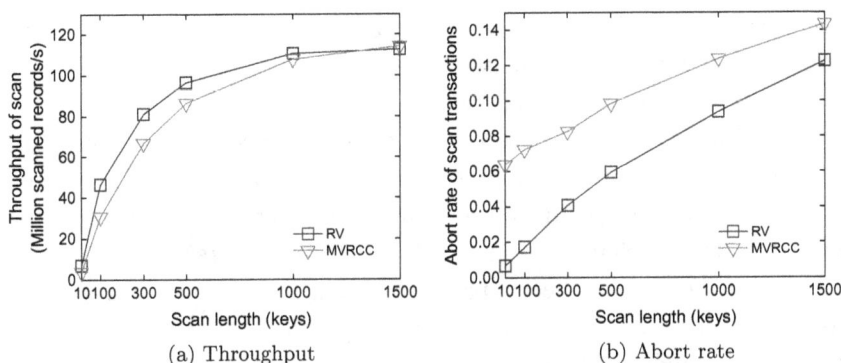

(a) Throughput   (b) Abort rate

Figure 3.13: Comparison with MVRCC.

last scanned range) are usually not fully covered. RV uses predicates with start and end keys to precisely describe the scanned scope of boundary ranges. At the validation phase, RV examines whether the updated keys satisfy the predicate. In MVRCC, the boundary ranges are treated as fully scanned ranges, and thus it causes more false aborts.

We implement MVRCC in DB×1000 and make a comparison with RV using the hybrid YCSB workload. The number of the logical ranges is 16384 for both MVRCC and RV. The scan performance is presented in Figure 3.13(a). As we can see, the performance of RV is 51% higher than MVRCC when the scan length covers 100 keys and 12% higher when the scan length covers 500 keys. When the scan length exceeds more than 1000 keys, RV and MVRCC have similar performance. Figure 3.13(b) demonstrates that the abort rate of MVRCC is always higher than that of RV because of inaccurate detection of the transaction conflicts in boundary logical ranges.

3.7 Related Work

3.7.1 Locking-based concurrency control

2PL, regarded as pessimistic concurrency control method, has been widely implemented in database systems[b] [41,67]. To ensure serializability, it

---

[b]MySQL Cluster. http://www.mysql.com/products/cluster/.

acquires read or write locks on the data items or predicates at the first phase. After the transaction is committed or aborted, 2PL releases all requested locks in the second phase.

The hierarchy locking technique as a restricted form of predicate locking is used in some popular databases (e.g., MySQL (see footnote b), DB2 [41], PostgreSQL [67]) to guarantee the atomicity of range queries and thus avoid phantom abnormality. The multi-granularity locking protocol [31], as the theory basis for hierarchy locking, reduces the locking overhead in the case of scanning too many records by only requesting a high-level lock on the table or page object. For a key-range scan operation, hierarchy locking approach lacks of efficient scheme for accurate conflict detection between the course-grain lockable objects and the exact scanned scope. To protect a scanned key-range from being modified, next-key locking not only requests to lock the records within this range but also the interval between the adjacent keys [65]. Next-key locking has inaccurate conflict detection only at the boundary of key-range. It is not friendly with large scan operation as the overhead of locking so many keys can be highly expensive. Recently, under the architecture of separating concurrency control from data storage, a multi-version range concurrency control algorithm is proposed in Deuteronomy [59] which uses timestamp ordering to support range resources and prevent the phantom problem.

The scalability problem of locking-based concurrency control in main memory database systems with multi-cores received much attention in recent years [39,42,77,101]. The author of [39] introduced a speculative lock inheritance mechanism to transfer the hot database locks directly from one transaction to another transaction without the intervention of lock manager. A lightweight locking scheme was proposed to align the lock information with the record in order to reduce the overhead from centralized locking manager [77]. The author of [42] redesigned the lock manager to support staged allocation and deallocation of locks which is more friendly to multi-cores. The author of [101] leverages the lock contention to reorder those high-contention queries such that the highly contentious records are accessed as later as possible.

3.7.2 Optimistic concurrency control

Compared to locking-based concurrency control, the OCC mechanism has no performance hotspots at the read phase because the transaction is executed in the completely optimistical way. However, the validation and write phases execute in a relatively pessimistic manner. In the setting of multi-cores, it still has challenge of scaling out the serializable committing protocol. Silo [93] is based on a single version OCC schema. In the validation phase, it adopts time-based epochs to avoid the centralized bottleneck of generating serialization point. For the range query, Silo introduces a lightweight phantom detecting method by checking the version of B-Tree nodes which cover the scanned range, but it still needs to maintain all the scanned records and re-scan them before commit. Compared to Silo, our approach validates the records recently committed by other concurrent transactions, and avoid the high validation cost caused by re-scanning. The recently proposed TicToc [103] also gives up the centralized timestamp allocation and uses a data-driven method to derive the reasonable commit timestamp according to the timestamps of its modified records.

OCC protocol is believed to perform better than the pessimistic concurrency control under the low-contention workload, and cannot work well in high-contention workload. The mostly-optimistic concurrency control (MOCC) [96] combines the pessimistic locking method with OCC to reduce the transaction aborts and enhances the performance on highly contentious and dynamic workloads. MOCC proposed a queue-based reader–writer lock on parallel machines to support scalable locking mechanism. Transaction abort and restart is a limited option to resolve transaction conflicts, and thus it is worthy to reduce the abort rate. BCC [105] reduces the false aborts of transactions by detecting data dependency patterns with low overhead and improves the performance for high-contention workloads. Instead of simply aborting a transaction when its validation fails, the authors of Ref. [100] introduced a transaction healing mechanism to restore the non-serializable operations and heal inconsistent states caused by transaction conflicts.

Multiple version concurrency control (MVCC) has a particularly attractive feature that the write and read operations don't block each other. Hekaton [56] designed multi-version OCC (MVOCC) scheme and it has been reported that MVOCC has better performance compared to the scheme of combing multiple version storage with the locking-based concurrency control. To ensure serializability, in the validation phase, Hekaton checks whether the version of each record in the read set has been changed. For range queries, Hekaton re-scans the range to detect serializability violation and prevent the phantom problem.

HyPer is a high-performance database systems towards OLTP&OLAP mixed workloads [71]. It proposed a fast MVCC protocol to achieve good scan performance and also guarantee the serializability for the heterogeneous workload. Each transaction keeps read predicates on its predicate tree. Instead of detecting conflicts by checking the records in the read set, HyPer validates the predicate tree against the writes from other recently committed transactions. In this chapter, the validation strategy is referred to as GWV. GWV may not be applicable for the update-intensive workloads, where the validating transaction needs to detect conflicts by checking massive updates from a large number of concurrent transactions. In this situation, GWV restricts the conflict detection within logical ranges and thus reduces the count of transactions to be validated.

3.8 Conclusion

In this chapter, we emphasize that the existing popular OCC protocols used by in-memory databases are not optimal for the emerging heterogeneous workloads including point accesses as well as key-range scan operation. To address the challenge, we proposed a scalable ROCC scheme. It adopts the RV method, which uses the logical ranges to track the potential conflicting transactions and tries its best to limit the number of transactions to be validated. ROCC not only can avoid the prohibitive cost of re-scanning the large key-range, but it also does not require system-wide lookup for overlapping transaction. Our evaluation results demonstrate that ROCC can maintain high performance for short and large key-range scan transactions with serializability guarantee. In addition, ROCC provides better scalability on transaction processing with key-range scan operation and achieves comparable or superior overall performance in high-contention workloads.

4

Global Snapshot Isolation

4.1 Introduction

Replication is a key technique to achieve better scalability, availability and fault-tolerance in distributed systems, and its challenge is how to maintain the consistency between replicas. Many traditional DBMS products adopt primary-backup technique including *eager* or *lazy* schemes to replicate writes from a primary replica node to multiple backup nodes [30]. Eager replication has bad performance as the transaction can't be committed until its updates have been synchronously installed at all replicas. On the other hand, lazy replication sacrifices consistency, especially when the primary crashed and failed to replicate the logs of committed transaction. Replication protocols based on group communication presented by Kemme and Alonso [48] utilize total order broadcast primitives to ensure that updates are applied in the same order at all replicas. This technique can maintain the scalability of replication without violating consistency. However, the cost of its synchronization is still high due to the fact that a write is synchronized to all replicas in the group [98]. Furthermore, systems using group communication need to rely on an external highly available component due to the assumption that only a primary group is able to continue when the network is partitioned [46].

Paxos [54] has been widely used to build a highly available and consistent distributed system containing unreliable servers and asynchronous network. Therefore, using Paxos to replicate log is a popular choice in database systems, such as IBM's Spinnaker [82], Google's MegaStore [3] and Spanner. To reduce network overhead, Spanner replicates transactional log entries using multi-Paxos [55] in which a replica is elected to be the leader and the first phase in the classic Paxos is not necessary. In common cases, the leader replica commits a log entry after synchronizing it to a majority of Paxos members referred to as followers. Then, the leader notifies the followers of the latest commit information in the later leader–follower communication.

Snapshot isolation (SI) [4], a well-known multi-version concurrency control (MVCC) method, is widely available in many DBMS engines like Oracle, PostgreSQL and Microsoft SQL Server due to the non-blocking read processing. In the past decade, there have been many research works [7,8,14,20,43,61] focusing on the combination of SI and various replication schemes for distributed database systems. Strong snapshot isolation (strong-SI), which is regarded as one-copy SI, is friendly to application programmers, and is also used to naturally resolve the problem of transaction inversions in lazy replication [61]. It needs a strongly consistent read to guarantee the *recency property* from the strong consistency. Unfortunately, it is still non-trivial to achieve strongly consistent read when reading the data from any replica. Paxos-based protocols require a write to be visible only when its corresponding log entry has persisted in a majority of Paxos members. There is a non-negligible data version difference between the leader and follower nodes since the leader always commits a transaction first and then informs the followers to commit. Until the log is replayed in the followers, the latest updated data cannot be observed from these replicas. This procedure leads to the result that the data on the follower nodes are less fresh than that on the leader. If the application requires strongly consistent read, the database system must process read operations only in the leader which owns the latest state of database. In this case, the leader node has the potential risk of suffering from overload and this makes a significant impact on the throughput and response time. Therefore, many system designs relax the strong consistency requirement to achieve high performance via weakly consistent read.

In this chapter, we propose early log replay (ELR) algorithm, by which we can achieve efficient snapshot isolation (ESI) in Paxos-replicated database systems. The main goal of our approach is to avoid read blocking and read failure in the conventional implementation of strong-SI. To decrease the overhead of leader replica, we also present an adaptive timestamp allocation (ATA) mechanism. ATA effectively reduces the number of timestamp requests to the leader. The following is the list of our main contributions:

- We give a basic implementation of SI in a Paxos-replicated database system, analyze its transaction read execution and figure out the root causes of read blocking, read failure and leader overloading.
- We propose ELR mechanism to implement an ESI in Paxos-replicated database systems. ELR can avoid read blocking effectively. To guarantee the correctness of data, we give the recovery mechanism for ELR.
- We present ATA to reduce the leader's overhead imposed by frequently processing timestamp requests. ATA allows the leader's timestamp to be embedded into response messages (e.g., write/commit response messages). By means of ATA, the leader only handles timestamp requests in a few rare cases.
- We implement the ESI in an open source database system OceanBase. Experimental results demonstrate the effectiveness of our method in terms of scalability and throughput.

The reminder of the chapter is organized as follows: The background of SI is introduced in Section 4.2. We give and analyze SI in Paxos-replicated database systems in Section 4.3. Section 4.4 presents an efficient version of SI for Paxos replication systems. In Section 4.5, we introduce the ATA, and experimental results are presented in Section 4.6. Finally, related work and conclusions are presented in Sections 4.7 and 4.8, respectively.

4.2 Background

SI, which is one kind of MVCC, was proposed by Berenson *et al.* [4]. Under SI, the transaction manager assigns a transaction T a start timestamp ($T.sts$) when it receives a start transaction request. The transaction T reads data from the latest snapshot of database containing the data committed before its start timestamp. When a transaction T is ready to commit, it gets a commit timestamp ($T.cts$) which is larger than any existing start timestamps or commit timestamps.

It is not straightforward to extend SI, originally defined over a centralized database, to replicated database systems. The main reason is the "latest" snapshot is not well defined in the distributed environment. Generalized snapshot isolation (GSI) allows the transaction to execute over an old local snapshot of database [26]. As the read may not get the last committed write in GSI, it violates the recency guarantee of strong consistency [2].

To achieve the same SI semantics of centralized DBMS, a simple approach is to globally order all transactions to maintain the partial order of operations from different clients. In other words, when a database replica receives a start transaction request from a client, it ensures the latest snapshot is allocated to this transaction. This is referred to as the concept of strong-SI, and the formal definition is as follows [20]:

Definition 4.1 (Strong-SI). A history $\mathcal{H}$ of transactions satisfies strong-SI, if it has the following property: for any pair of transactions T_i and T_j, if the database replica receives the commit of T_i before the start of T_j, then $T_i.cts \leq T_j.sts$.

Owing to the recency guarantee, strong-SI in distributed database systems is also regarded as one-copy SI [61], where the effect of transactions performed on the database replicas is the same as that in a single centralized database. Strong-SI is friendly to application developers. Therefore, in this chapter, our target is to implement strong-SI in a Paxos-replicated database system.

4.3 SI in Paxos-replicated Database Systems

4.3.1 System architecture

For ease of description, we assume that the replicated database is a main-memory key-value store. The simplified architecture contains two components:

- **Request Processing Nodes (RP-Node):** RP-Node is the bridge between the clients and the database. Its task is to parse the SQL, generate the logical/physical plan and forward the generated plan to the transaction processing nodes (TP-Nodes). It should be noted that RP-Node is stateless.

- **Transaction Processing Nodes (TP-Node):** A set of TP-nodes constitute a Paxos group, and each one maintains a full copy of the database. TP-node is responsible for concurrency control and log replication. To reduce the consensus cost, the group adopting multi-Paxos consists of only one leader as primary replica and multiple followers as backups.

4.3.2 Transaction execution

In the architecture described above, all start-transaction, read/write and commit-transaction requests need to be processed by the leader TP-node, which is responsible for transaction scheduling and log replication. When the leader receives the commit-transaction request of an update transaction, it generates a log entry including the transaction's writes and then uses Paxos-based replication protocol to synchronize the log to other TP-nodes. As shown in Figure 4.1, the classical Paxos-based log replication is divided into two phases, which are as follows:

Phase 1: The leader TP-Node sends the log entry to other TP-nodes. After the leader confirms the log has been successfully replicated to the majority of TP-Nodes, it can commit this transaction and then respond to the client.

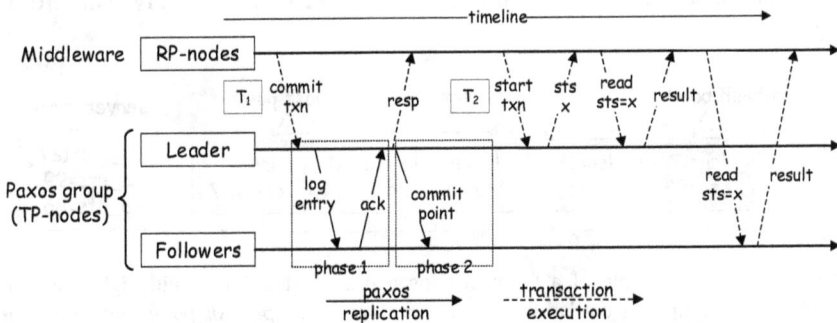

Figure 4.1: Transaction execution in a Paxos-replicated database system.

Phase 2: The leader firstly updates its local *commit point*, and then asynchronously notifies other TP-Node of the latest committed logs in the later communication. It should be noted that the commit point is represented by log sequence number (LSN), and log entries are persisted and replayed in the order of LSN. When a follower TP-Node receives the latest commit point from leader, it can refresh its local commit point and replay these logs with LSN prior to and including this commit point.

As described in Phase 2, the data committed at leader is not immediately visible at follower until it receives the commit point and completes the log replaying. To obtain the scalability property of replication, after a transaction gets its *start timestamp* from the leader, it is expected that subsequent read requests can be forwarded to leader or followers, as illustrated in Figure 4.1. To handle a read request under strong-SI, a follower needs to hold a multi-version storage engine, and a read operation of T_j can access data only when the replica includes all T_i's writes, where $T_i.cts \leq T_j.sts$. In this work, the *commit timestamp* of a transaction is embedded into its log entry. The state of followers reflecting data recency is represented by three variables. (1) *flush_cts* (*f_cts*): The commit timestamp in the last log entry flushed by this follower TP-Node; (2) *commit_cts* (*c_cts*): The commit timestamp in the log entry whose LSN is equal to the latest received commit point; (3) *publish_cts* (*p_cts*): The commit timestamp in the log entry with maximal LSN in all replayed log entries.

To further demonstrate how the state of a follower influences transaction execution, an example is presented in Figure 4.2. The commit point and last point in the follower are 19 and 21, respectively. Therefore,

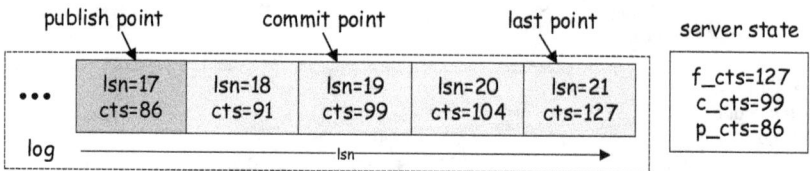

publish point	commit point	last point	server state

| ... | lsn=17
cts=86 | lsn=18
cts=91 | lsn=19
cts=99 | lsn=20
cts=104 | lsn=21
cts=127 | f_cts=127
c_cts=99
p_cts=86 |

log ————————————————————lsn————————————————————→

Figure 4.2: An example of a follower's log and state. The boxes with light gray are used to denote the log entries that are not replayed. The *publish point* and *last point* are used to denote LSN of the last replayed entry and LSN of the last persisted entry, respectively.

the corresponding c_cts and f_cts are 99 and 127, respectively. Since the log entries before LSN 18 have been replayed, p_cts is equal to 86. Based on the follower's state, there are four cases on how a read request of transaction T is handled according to strong-SI, and these are as follows:

Case 1: $f\_cts < T.sts$. The follower realizes that the RP-node requests a non-existent snapshot. *In other words, its log lags behind leader's.* Therefore, it immediately returns a failure response message.

Case 2: $c\_cts < T.sts \leq f\_cts$. This indicates that the follower is waiting for the latest commit point from the leader. To avoid waiting a long time, a failure response for the request is returned directly.

Case 3: $p\_cts < T.sts \leq c\_cts$. The follower learns that the expected version of data will be available soon. Accordingly, *the request is blocked until $p\_cts \geq T.sts$*. Finally, the follower returns a response message with expected data.

Case 4: $T.sts \leq p\_cts$. The follower directly gets the data of expected version from local database snapshot and returns a successful response including the data to the RP-node.

If the followers handle read requests according to the four cases, it is referred to as the *basic* implementation of strong-SI in Paxos-replicated DBMS. Although the simplest method to achieve the Strong-SI is to let the leader TP-Node handle all read/write operations, it loses much scalability. Even under the basic implementation of Strong-SI, the read requests handled by followers may still be failed or blocked. We make an analysis on this problem in the next subsection.

4.3.3 Problem analysis

Recall that Paxos-based replication has two properties: (1) The leader can commit a log entry if it receives a majority of acknowledgments. In other words, a follower TP-node may not have the latest log. In Figure 4.3, the TP-node 3 does not have the entry with LSN 22. (2) The follower can replay a log entry only when receiving the commit information about the entry. In Figure 4.3, the commit point is sent asynchronously to the follower TP-node 2. The visibility of a write in the TP-node 2 is always later than that in the leader. To guarantee

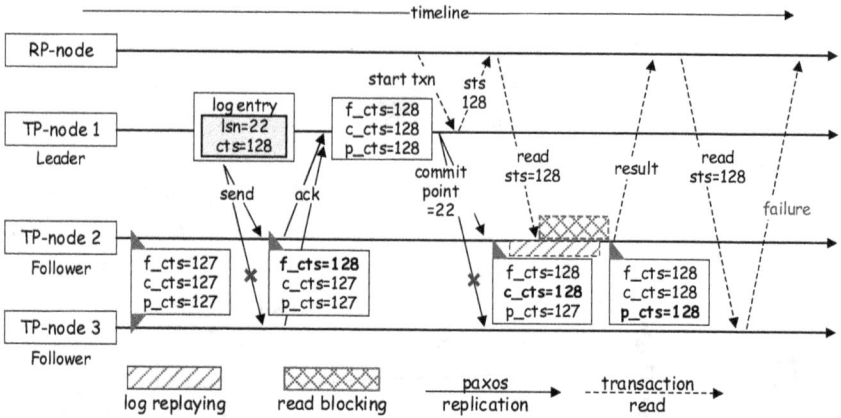

Figure 4.3: An example of transaction read with blocking or failure. This is 3-way Paxos replication system, where TP-node 1 is the leader. Assuming that all variables (i.e., f_cts, c_cts and p_cts) in each TP-node's server state are 127 at the beginning.

the recency property, a transaction is assigned a newest start timestamp from the leader TP-node. As shown in Figure 4.3, when the leader receives a start-transaction request, it assigns the $p\_cts(128)$ as the *start timestamp* to the transaction. We summarize the issues in the execution of transaction read as follows:

Issue 1: A transaction read can be rejected by a follower. In Figure 4.3, the RP-node sends a read request of a transaction T with $sts(128)$ to TP-node 3. Since $f\_cts(127) < T.sts(128)$, the read is rejected directly by TP-node 3.

Issue 2: A transaction read can be blocked in a follower. In Figure 4.3, we find that a read request of a transaction T with $sts(128)$ is blocked by TP-node 2. Although TP-node 2 has the latest log, the log is being replayed and the data of expected version is invisible.

Issue 3: Under Strong-SI, the start-transaction request of each transaction is always forwarded to the leader replica. Therefore, the leader may be faced with a large number of requests, which can negatively impact the system's performance.

Both Issues 1 and 2 decrease the read performance of Paxos-replicated database systems. To address these issues, we introduce a design of ESI utilizing ELR mechanism. For Issue 3, we present ATA for read-only transactions in Section 4.5.

4.4 Efficient Snapshot Isolation

4.4.1 Overview

We have introduced a basic implementation of SI in Paxos-replicated database system in Section 4.3. In this section, we present an *efficient* version. To implement an ESI, our design target has two sides: (1) An RP-node is required to forward a read request to the TP-node having the latest log; (2) A follower can replay its local log without waiting leader's commit point.

An example of transaction read in ESI is illustrated in Figure 4.4. For the first target, the leader responds with a message including the available followers' information (TP-node 2). This is because the leader ensures that TP-node 2 has the latest log. RP-node can forward subsequent read requests according to the response. For the second target, when the follower TP-node 2 receives a log entry with *commit timestamp* ($cts = 128$) from the leader, it replays the entry immediately without waiting for the corresponding commit point. Then, the follower can update its p_cts to 128 after replaying successfully. Owing to the efforts for both targets, a transaction read with $sts(128)$ can be processed without blocking in TP-node 2.

The first target can be easily achieved. To guarantee the correctness of implementation for the second target, we introduce ELR mechanism in the following subsections.

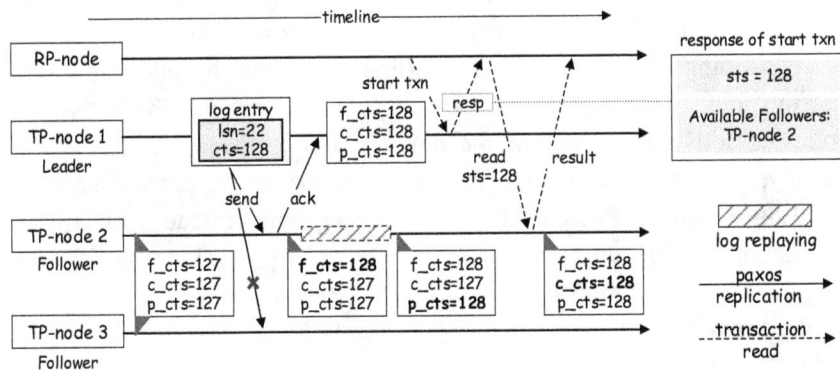

Figure 4.4: An example of transaction read avoiding failure and blocking. All variables (i.e., f_cts, c_cts and p_cts) in each TP-node's server state are 127 at start.

4.4.2 Early log replay

Owing to the multi-version storage of SI for main-memory database, each object can utilize a committed list (*c_list*) to store multiple versions in the order of committed timestamps [99]. In a follower replica, each version—which contains a value and a timestamp (*cts* of the transaction creating the version)—can be constructed from the corresponding log entry. We design a *centralized uncommitted list* (*uc_list*) to store the pointers to all of uncommitted versions. *uc_list* is used for data recovery when failure happens (see Section 4.4.4).

To safely replay log without commit point in followers, ELR decomposes the conventional log replay into two phases: *early log replay* and *log commit*. The pseudocode of functions used by ELR is shown in Algorithm 4.1. Assuming that a log entry *e* contains only one updated object. Accordingly, we use *e.key* and *e.value* to denote the object's key and value, respectively. Next, we describe in a detailed manner the transition of follower state using ELR.

When a follower receives a log entry message from the leader, it invokes the function `LogReceiver`. The function flushes the entry into the non-volatile storage and then refreshes the local f_cts from the log entry (lines 2–3). Next, the follower appends the entry to a queue (line 4), which stores the log entries that are ready to replay. We call it *log_queue*. Finally, the follower responds to the leader (line 5).

Early Log Replay Phase: There is a thread running `Early LogReplayer`, which is responsible for ELR phase. If the thread gets a log entry from the *log_queue*, it parses the entry and gets the corresponding object from the local (line 11). Then, it generates a new version and appends it to the object's *c_list* (lines 12–13). Next, the follower adds the pointer of the new version to the *uc_list* (line 14). Finally, it updates the local p_cts using the *cts* of the entry (line 15).

Log Commit Phase: There is a background thread which is in charge of the log commit phase. It periodically invokes the function `LogCommitter` using c_cts. It gets the head in the *uc_list*. If the *cts* of the version is not larger than c_cts, the follower removes the pointer from the *uc_list* (lines 20–21).

Algorithm 4.1: Early log replay algorithm

---

1 <u>Function</u> LogReceiver(*entry*)

2   flush *entry* to disk;

3     $f\_cts = entry.cts$;

4   log_queue.enqueue(*entry*);

5   response to the leader;

6 end

    /* early log replay phase   */

7 <u>Function</u> EarlyLogReplayer()

8   while *true* do

9   if ¬*log_queue*.isEmpty() then

10           $entry = log\_queue$.dequeue();

11   obj = getObjectByKey(*entry.key*);

12           $version$ = new Version(*entry.value, entry.cts*);

13           $obj.c\_list$.add(*version*);

14   uc_list.add(*version*);

15           $p\_cts = \max(p\_cts, entry.cts)$;

16   end

17   end

18 end

    /* log commit phase   */

19 <u>Function</u> LogCommitter(*c_cts*)

20   while ¬*uc_list*.isEmpty() ∧ *c_cts* > *uc_list*.get(0).cts do

21   uc_list.remove(0);

22   end

23 end

4.4.3 Transaction read execution

When a follower TP-node receives a read request, it needs to return the data satisfying the expected version. This processing flow is similar to that described in Section 4.3.2, excepting that the follower's c_cts is not used to determine whether this read request can be processed. Since a read is forwarded to a follower having the latest log, it can be served without blocking due to ELR mechanism.

We note that a read request contains the *start timestamp*, which represents a required snapshot. In other words, the log entry whose timestamp is not larger than the *start timestamp* is committed. *Therefore, the follower can update local c_cts to the request's sts and invoke the function* LogCommitter *to handle the versions in the uncommitted list* uc_list.

4.4.4 Recovery

If the leader TP-Node is corrupted, Paxos group will leverage election mechanism to achieve automatic fault tolerance. A typical method is that a TP-node wins the election if its logs are not older than a majority of TP-nodes. When a new leader is elected, any component in the system needs to take efforts to guarantee strong-SI services:

- **New Leader:** The new leader must do some work for takeover. It is required to ensure that all writes in the log are committed, i.e., it synchronized local log to at least a majority of TP-nodes. After log synchronization, it can empty the *uc_list* and apply all log entries. Finally, the leader returns to normal and can receive request from RP-nodes.
- **Follower:** When a TP-node detects that a new leader is not itself, it becomes a follower and needs to take some measures to ensure the validation of local data. Due to invalid versions in the *uc_list* (i.e., a version does not exist in the new leader), the follower needs to ask the leader to check the local log to find the invalid log entries. Then, the follower traverses the *uc_list*, removes the pointer of committed version directly and deletes the invalid versions in the objects' *c_list*.
- **RP-node:** When an RP-node is informed of the crash of leader, it notes that all writes are blocked until the new leader is elected and returns to normal. On the other hand, the RP-node can issue these unfinished read-only transaction to other TP-node's.

If a follower TP-Node recovers from a failure, it only checks the local log and applies the correct entries to local due to the main memory storage engine.

4.5 Adaptive Timestamp Allocation

Recall from Section 4.3 that an RP-node needs to ask the leader to get a latest *start timestamp* for each start-transaction request from the clients. As a result, the leader may be faced with tremendous pressure. In this section, we introduce ATA mechanism to reduce the number of timestamp requests.

Note that if a transaction is a read-only one, it doesn't need to be registered in the leader replica. Therefore, in order to reduce the overhead caused by the *start timestamp* requests in the leader, we can adopt batch processing technique in the RP-node for the read-only transactions. More specifically, the RP-node uses a buffer to keep a batch of start-transaction requests from clients and send only one timestamp request to the leader. The RP-node asks the leader for a new start timestamp every d milliseconds. In real applications, it is difficult to determine which is the optimal value of d. If d is too small, the leader will receive an enormous amount of start requests; if d is too large, the delay of clients' requests will be increased.

The idea of ATA is to allow the RP-node to embed the timestamp request into a write or commit request issued by other transaction. Now we analyze the cost of timestamp request in terms of how many requests are sent to the leader. We assume that the arrival time of read/write request is uniformly distributed, and an RP-node needs $1000/d$ timestamp requests per second. In one second, an RP-node receives n requests. If the percentage of writes is w in the workload, there are $n \cdot w$ writes per second that need to be forwarded to the leader. Equation (4.1) shows the number of timestamp requests sent to the leader.

$$f(d, n, w) = \max\left(0, \frac{1000}{d} - n \cdot w\right) \qquad (4.1)$$

Assume that $w = 5\%$, which is a typical value in the read-intensive workload. According to Equation (4.1), we can see that if the extra timestamp requests are not required, the optimal d can be set to less than 4 milliseconds when $n >= 5,000$. If n is small, it indicates that the overhead of the leader is not heavy. In this kind of case, the RP-node can send additional timestamp requests to the leader to further decrease the delay of clients' requests. It is clear that the average delay of a client's request is incremented by $d/2$ milliseconds. We can see that if $n = 10,000$, the request delay is only incremented by 1 millisecond.

Although the leader TP-Node embeds its state of related timestamps into a sequence of message for responding many write/commit requests, it should be noted that not all returned timestamps can be served as the start-timestamp of a transaction. *To guarantee the recency property of strong-SI, only the returned timestamps can be taken as a valid start timestamp of a transaction if this message is responded to the write/commit request sent by the RP-Node after the start-transaction request arrived.* Therefore, the RP-node is required to record the sent time, $send\_ts$, for each request. In order to efficiently allocate the start timestamps, RP-node utilizes two components *pending list* and *sts manager*, which are illustrated in Figure 4.5. The FIFO *pending list* is used to store the pending read-only transactions in the order of their arrival timestamps. We can see that there are four transactions a, b, c and d in Figure 4.5, which are waiting for the suitable start timestamps. The *sts manager* manages the latest $send\_ts$ of a message whose response is received by the RP-node and the p_cts in the corresponding response. More specifically, when an RP-node receives a response from the leader, it will refresh the values in the *sts manager* if the $send\_ts$ of corresponding send message is greater. In Figure 4.5, the RP-node receives the response of

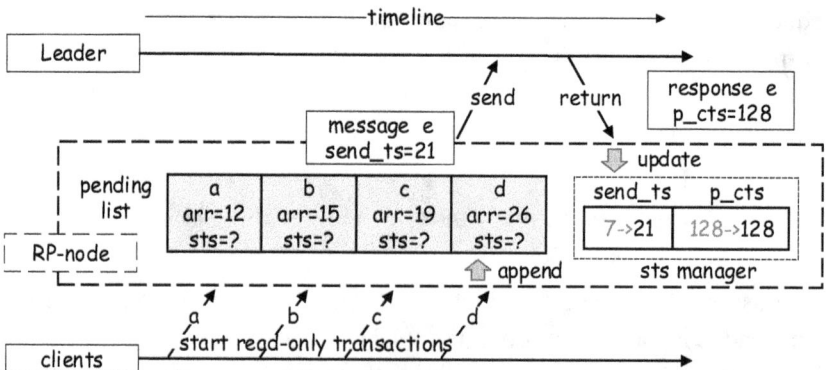

Figure 4.5: An example of assigning start timestamps for clients' read-only transactions without violating recency guarantee. A read-only transaction is allocated an arrival time (arr) and appended into *pending list*. Then it is waiting for a suitable start timestamp (sts), which is triggered by the update of *sts manager*.

message e from the leader, and then updates $send\_ts$ and p_ts to 21 and 128, respectively. This triggers an event that the RP-node allocates the $p\_ts(128)$ to transactions in the *pending list*, whose arrival timestamps are not larger than the $send\_ts(21)$, i.e., the transactions a, b and c.

There is a background thread which is responsible for checking the *sts manager* periodically. If the values in the manager are not updated in d milliseconds, the thread will send a start timestamp request to the leader.

4.6 Experiments

We implemented ESI in OceanBase 0.4.2[a], which is a scalable open source RDBMS developed by Alibaba. We conducted an experimental study to evaluate the performance of the proposed ESI. The experimental setup and the benchmark used in this evaluation are given below.

Cluster platform: We deployed a 3-way replication database system including RP-nodes and TP-nodes on a cluster of 18 machines, and each machine is equipped with a 2-socket Intel Xeon E5606 @2.13GHz (a total of 8 physical cores), 96GB RAM and 100GB SSD while running CentOS version 6.5.

Competitors: We use **SINGLE** to denote the system containing only one TP-node without any log replication. Its experimental results will be helpful for understanding the behavior with other strategies. We use **BASIC** and **ESI** to denote the implementation of basic version and efficient version of SI, respectively. The framework of GSI, which allows a transaction read over an arbitrary old data version, is denoted as **WEAK**.

Benchmark: First, we adopt YCSB [17] to evaluate our implementation. We use the workloads YCSB A and B (abbr.workload-A and workload-B), which have a read/write ratio of 50/50 and 95/5, respectively, and each transaction contains only one operation. Second, to investigate the performance of complicated transaction workload, we use five read/write operations to generate a transaction with multiple operations. The size of each update is about 100 bytes.

---

[a]OceanBase website. https://github.com/alibaba/oceanbase/.

4.6.1 Scalability

Figure 4.6(a) illustrates the system throughput over an increasing number of clients under the workload-B with read-intensive operations. Because all requests were forwarded to the single node, the performance of SINGLE is the worst. Owing to the serviceability of followers, WEAK has the highest throughput, compared with SINGLE by about 2.5× when the number of clients was more than 600. Recall from Section 4.3.3 that there are some issues in the basic version of GSI. Therefore, the results of BASIC was about two-thirds that of WEAK. Since an uncommitted write can be published in ELR, a read could be processed quickly without blocking in any alive replica. This advantage makes the performance of ESI very similar to WEAK. Accordingly, ESI maintains the goodness of replication under read intensive workload.

Figure 4.6(b) shows the results under workload-A with write-intensive operations. The trend of the results is similar to that in Figure 4.6(a). Due to the overhead for synchronizing a large amount of updates log by the leader node, the throughput of the 3-way replication system was limited and less than SINGLE when the number of clients is more than 640. It is worthwhile to note that although ESI provides strong-SI, it has a similar performance to WEAK. Furthermore, we also observed that ESI outperforms BASIC, since the read requests are always not blocked in the followers adopting ELR.

In the transaction workload, a read-only transaction contains multiple read operations, as ESI reduces the timestamp requests dramatically and

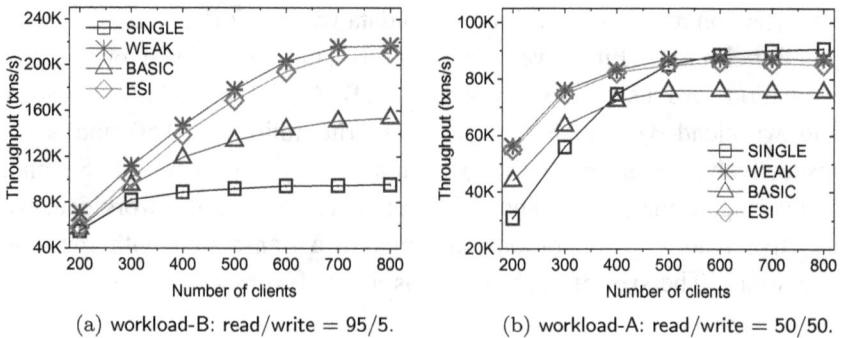

(a) workload-B: read/write = 95/5.   (b) workload-A: read/write = 50/50.

Figure 4.6: Throughput for YCSB workloads.

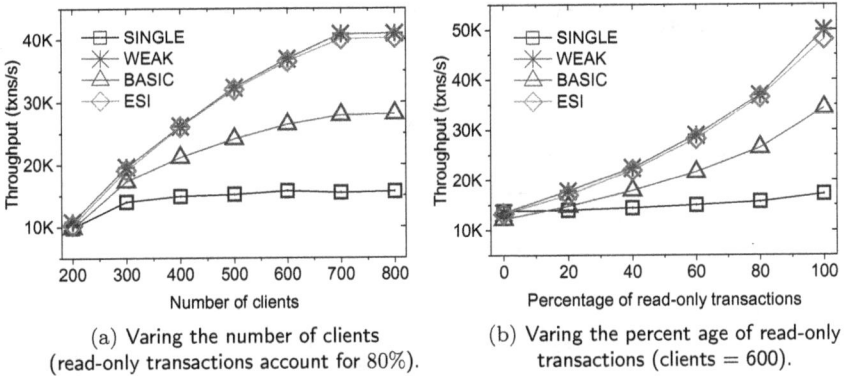

(a) Varing the number of clients
(read-only transactions account for 80%).

(b) Varing the percent age of read-only
transactions (clients = 600).

Figure 4.7: Throughput for transaction workloads, where each read-only transaction contains five read operations and each update transaction contains three reads and two writes.

allows the RP-nodes to quickly forward **read** operations to a qualified follower node. Thus, the results of **ESI** are nearly the same as that of **WEAK**, which is shown in Figure 4.7.

4.6.2 Effectiveness

To investigate the effectiveness of ELR mechanism, we compare **ESI** against **BASIC**. Recall from Section 4.3.2 that p_cts is used to denote the latest server state a client can access. Assuming that the leader ℓ and the follower f update their p_cts to the same timestamp at physical time t_ℓ and t_f, respectively. We use the result of $(t_f - t_\ell)$ to denote the time gap between the same visible state of leader l and one follower f.

Figure 4.8 shows the visibility difference of all p_cts's between a follower and the leader over 120 seconds for the workload-B. The number of clients is fixed to 240, where the system can output stable results. We can see that the visibility difference of **BASIC** exceeds 50 milliseconds, which suggests that a read expecting a latest version may not be satisfied in followers. And the visibility difference of **ESI** was close to the zero, which indicates that a log entry has been replayed successfully in followers when it finishes the commit phase in the leader. ELR ensures that the expected data can be returned immediately for the transaction read at the follower replica.

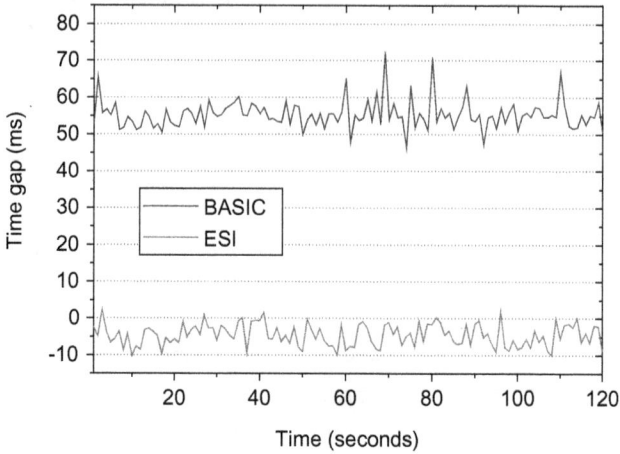

Figure 4.8: Effectiveness of ELR: workload-A.

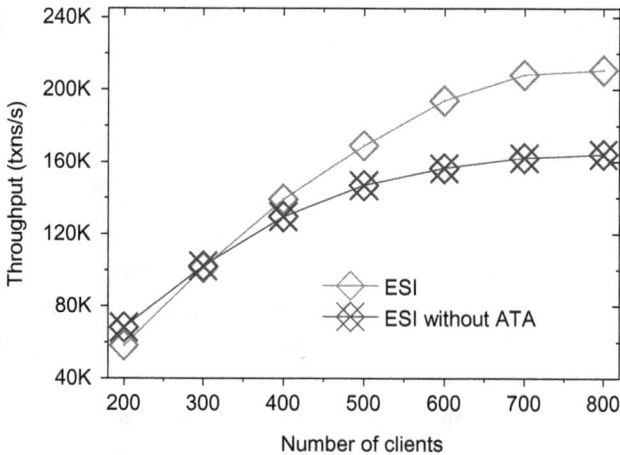

Figure 4.9: Effectiveness of ATA: workload-B.

To investigate the effectiveness of ATA, we evaluate the performance of ESI without ATA, where RP-nodes send a start timestamp request for each read. Figure 4.9 illustrates the experimental results under workload-B. It is clear that the delay of a start transaction request in RP-nodes may impact the system performance. We can see that ESI without ATA exceeds ESI when the workload is low (i.e., the leader

TP-node has the enough capacity to process each request). However, as the number of clients increases, the leader is faced with increasing overhead. When workload is high, due to the reduction of requests to the leader, ESI significantly outperforms ESI without ATA. Therefore, in the case of heavy workload, ATA has a positive effect on system performance.

4.7 Related Work

Replication: Replication is an effective mechanism to provide scalability, high availability and fault tolerance in distributed systems. State machine replication (SMR) [86], a fundamental approach to fault-tolerant services, can ensure that the replica is consistent with each other only if the operations are executed in the same order on all replicas. Eager or lazy replication [30] has been a standard criteria for database systems. But these schemes cannot satisfy the requirement of both performance and consistency. Kemme *et al.* [48] presented a replication protocol based on group communication, which can maintain the scalability of replication without violating consistency. However, the assumption that high-throughput network and an external highly available service are required limits the use of group communication. Wiesmann *et al.* [76] compared and summarized the replication techniques from database and distributed system communities.

    Snapshot Isolation for Replication: SI [4], which allows write-skew anomaly but offers greater performance, is widely available in DBMS engines like Oracle and PostgreSQL. In the past decade, there have been many research works [7,8,14,20,43,61] focusing on the combination of replication and SI for distributed database systems. Lin *et al.* [61] presented a middleware-based replication scheme which provides strongly global SI. Daudjee and Salem [20] showed how SI can be maintained in lazy replicated systems while taking full advantage of each replica's concurrency control. Jung *et al.* [43] proposed replicated serializable SI, which can guarantee 1-copy serializable global execution. ConfluxDB [14] determined a total SI order for update transactions over multiple master sites without requiring global coordination. Binnig *et al.* [7] further defined distributed SI and accordingly proposed a criteria to efficiently implement SI. To the best of our knowledge, there is no SI implementation over Paxos-replicated main-memory database systems.

Paxos replication: To provide highly available services, modern database systems often adopt Paxos protocol—which was first described by Lamport in Refs. [54,55]—to replicate data from primary to backup replicas. Raft [73] is a famous variant of Paxos, which is widely used in open-source databases. Google has developed MegaStore [3] and Spanner, which utilize Paxos for log replication. Spanner implements distributed transaction processing and provides external consistency based on TrueTime API. Nonetheless, the non-blocking transaction read can only be forwarded to the leader replica. Spinnaker [82] builds a scalable, consistent and highly available data store using Paxos-based replication. However, a read request processed by a backup node only offers weak consistency. Moraru *et al.* [68] introduced the method of Paxos quorum leases to allow strongly consistent local read be performed at replicas which are lease holders. The lease mechanisms have small negative impact on the availability.

Spanner implemented concurrency control mechanism and Paxos-based replication at different layers, and both of them have consistency requirements. To reduce the coordination cost, [69,106] consolidate concurrency and Paxos census to decrease the network round-trips.

4.8 Conclusion

In this chapter, we presented an ESI, an optimized implementation of strong-SI in Paxos-replicated database systems. By analyzing the transaction execution of basic version, we proposed two effective mechanisms for ESI, i.e., ELR and ATA. ELR avoids to block or fail the execution of transaction read in followers. ATA relieves the leader's overhead by reducing the number of timestamp requests sent to the leader. Experimental results demonstrate the effectiveness of ELR and ATA.

5

Log Replication

5.1 Introduction

Today's mission-critical enterprise applications require the back-end database system to provide high performance and high availability. The In-Memory Database (IMDB) is regarded as a high-performance OLTP database management system, and it is designed to make full use of the capabilities of hardware such as multi-core and large memory. Replication is the technique used for IMDB to support high availability. Different replication schemes have been developed for traditional centralized database systems using disks as main storage, and they are also natively integrated into Geo-distributed data stores [64,70].

There are two popular replication techniques: the asynchronous primary-backup replication (APR) and the quorum-based replication (QR). The asynchronous primary-backup replication provides fault-tolerance in traditional database systems (see footnote b of chapter 3), where a transaction is firstly committed at the primary and then its log is asynchronously propagated to replicas. Compared to the eager replication, a great advantage of asynchronous replication is that it has almost no overhead on transaction processing at the primary. However, one disadvantage of asynchronous replication is that there is inconsistency among the primary and the replicas. Another disadvantage is the risk of losing data when the primary is crashed. For example, if a transaction is committed at the primary but it has not been successfully replicated

89

to any backup replica, the committed data would be lost if the failure causes a permanent damage to the primary.

Distributed consensus protocols (e.g., Multi-Paxos [15], Raft [73], etc.) are the fundamental elements of QR mechanisms. Similar to the fully eager primary-backup replication, QR also achieves strong consistency and has better performance because it only requires the majority of replicas to respond to the primary, referred to as *partially synchronous replication*. Although the QR adopts consensus protocols to take more reasonable trade-offs between performance and consistency, they have only recently been accepted as a practical and efficient replication protocol for large-scale data stores [82,95,108].

QR protocols are the natural choice for replicating IMDB as a highly available and strongly consistent OLTP data store. Under the context of database replication, the common property of various quorum-based protocols is that committing a transaction requires its log to be replicated to and flushed to the non-volatile storages of the majority of replicas. To achieve read scalability and high availability, the replicas need to replay the committed transaction logs at a fast speed to keep up with the primary's state. However, we demonstrate that there are two technique obstacles of replicating IMDB under highly concurrent OLTP workloads.

The latency for synchronous replication: In the case of highly concurrent OLTP workloads, the primary IMDB node could generate transactional logs at a very fast rate. QR requires these enormous logs to be synchronously flushed to non-volatile storage of more than half the IMDB replica nodes. The latency for synchronous replication is the amount of time it takes for network transmission, log entry parsing and persistence in replica nodes. As the log processing at replicas is relatively slow, replicas are increasingly overwhelmed by the high-speed log stream sent by the primary. A straightforward solution is to limit transaction processing capacity of the primary IMDB and thus reduces the pressure of processing replicated logs for replicas. Obviously, this would significantly reduce the performance of primary IMDB.

Visibility gap (VGap): The classic QR requires the primary to send replicas the maximal committed log sequence number (MaxComLSN), and then replicas can commit and replay those logs with LSN smaller or equal to MaxComLSN. Replaying logs after receiving the specified

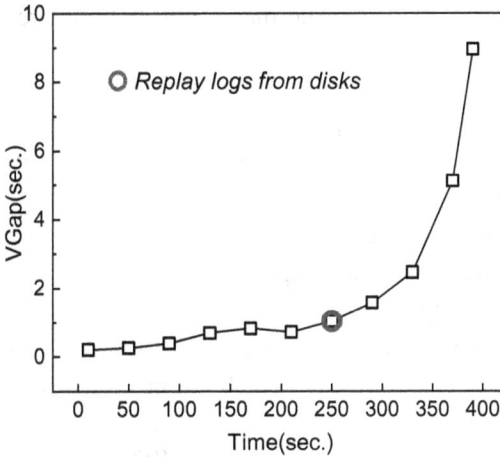

Figure 5.1: VGap in QR. Under highly concurrent workloads, the primary replicates so many logs to replicas that committed logs have not been replayed until they are erased from in-memory. Replaying logs from disks would lead to VGap grows larger.

MaxComLSN leads to the result that the committed data are visible at replicas are later than that at the primary, referred to as VGap. In addition, VGap would be larger when the primary is running under a heavy OLTP workload in QR. When receiving lots of transactional logs whose size exceeds the limited space of log buffer, the replica has the risk of reading flushed logs from the local storage for replay. In Figure 5.1, we demonstrate the VGap problem by running standard QR under a continued, heavy OLTP workload. Experimental results indicate that the log replay thread begins to read logs from disks as these logs are not cached in log buffer. In this case, the introduced I/O delay will result in more received logs having no chance of being replayed by reading them from in-memory log buffer. This would increasingly lead to a scenario that replicas lagged far behind the primary.

Replication latency and VGap can't cause serious issues for Geo-distributed database systems. The OLTP workload is uniformly divided and taken by each partitioned database node. Although each partition is also replicated by quorum-based protocols, the light OLTP workload on each partition would not introduce serious replication latency and VGap. In this chapter, we present an efficient QR framework, called as QuorumX, to optimize the replication performance for IMDB under highly concurrent OLTP workloads. The main contributions are summarized as follows:

- We design a *pipelined log persistence scheme* for hiding the latency of synchronous replication. To ameliorate the speed mismatch between the primary high-speed log generation and the replicas low-speed log processing, we propose an *adaptive log propagation algorithm* to adjust the frequency of sending logs, with a full consideration of the processing capacity of replicas.
- We introduce a safe and coordination-free log replay scheme without waiting for the MaxComLSN, which applies logs to memtables ahead of time to reduce the risk of VGap increasing.
- QuorumX has been implemented in Solar [92], an in-memory NewSQL database system that has been successfully deployed in Bank of Communications, one of the biggest commercial banks in China. Extensive experiments are conducted to evaluate QuorumX under different benchmarks.

The chapter is organized as follows. Section 5.2 describes our design motivations and overall architecture of QuorumX. Section 5.3 gives several detailed designs of pipelined log replication and adaptive log propagation algorithm. The log replaying scheme is described in Section 5.4. Section 5.5 presents the results of performance evaluation. Finally, in Section 5.6, we give an overview of related works, and Section 5.7 concludes this chapter.

5.2 Design Motivation

In this section, we illustrate design motivations by comparing APR with QR under the context of replicating IMDB, and then present the overall architecture of QuorumX.

5.2.1 Problem analysis

Figures 5.2 and 5.3 compare the processing steps in asynchronous primary-backup replication with those in QR. A transaction is committed at the primary, and then its log is asynchronously replicated to replicas.

Primary IMDB

start txn ①

txn latency   generate log ②

write log ③   **Replica IMDB**

commit txn ④

VGap   ·Send logs → ① replay log

② write log

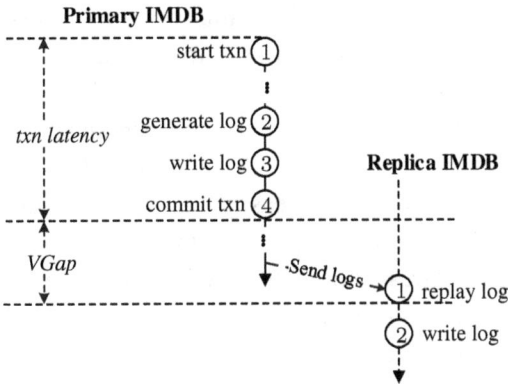

Figure 5.2: Asynchronous primary-backup replication.

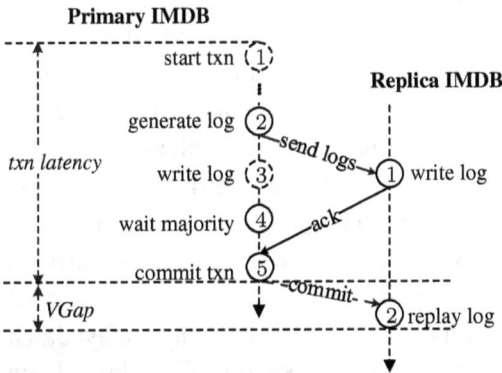

Primary IMDB

start txn ①   **Replica IMDB**

generate log ②   send logs

txn latency   write log ③   → ① write log

wait majority ④   ack

commit txn ⑤   commit

VGap   ② replay log

Figure 5.3: Quorum-based replication.

This indicates that asynchronous log replication has almost no effect on the commit latency of a transaction. However, as shown in Figure 5.3, the commit latency in QR is determined by the majority of replicas, and would increase because of synchronous log replication. The latency introduced by QR is high if the replica IMDB serially performs log parsing, log writing and replying to the primary. As a result, we make a thorough and careful design of speeding up log replication. In spite of this, the primary IMDB deployed on a modern multi-core server can handle massive transaction requests and generate logs at a very fast speed in a highly concurrent workload. In this case, the speed of replicating log at replicas with asynchronous primary-backup replication is not an important issue because it doesn't require the replica to quickly response to the primary, and therefore the primary remains high performance. While in QR, if the batch size and frequency of log propagation are not controlled, the replicas can easily be overwhelmed by this heavy workload. In this scenario, the pending logs at replica stay at working queue, and those corresponding transactions wait for a long time for being committed at the primary.

Existing solutions to VGap in the APR cannot apply to the QR. The VGap is defined as the time difference between the primary and replica for making the committed data be visible. Applications requiring real-time OLAP analysis always require there be only a small VGap between the primary and replicas. In APR, replicas could replay the received logs immediately without any coordination with the primary. Recent works for VGap in the synchronous replication have been done to reduce network overhead and accelerate parallel log replay [36,58,80]. However, in QR, the primary notifies replicas of the consensus decision of committing transactions by sending the current MaxComLSN. After receiving MaxComLSN, the replica nodes are agreed to replay logs with LSN no larger than MaxComLSN. Since it is expensive to read logs from disk for replay, the replicated and uncommitted logs need to reside in the memory for a period of time before being replayed. This motivated us to build an in-memory ring buffer to caching logs. Even so, in the case where the primary generates logs at a high speed, un-replayed logs in the buffer can be soon erased by the new arrivals. The replica still needs to read flushed logs from a disk for replaying, and would gradually lag behind the primary and produces larger VGap.

5.2.2 Overall architecture of QuorumX

Figure 5.4 shows the overall architecture of QuorumX. The replicated IMDB cluster contains one primary IMDB as a leader and more than two replica IMDBs as followers. All requests of read/write transactions are routed to the primary IMDB. After completing the execution of a transaction, the primary generates the corresponding transactional log,

Primary IMDB   **Replica IMDB**

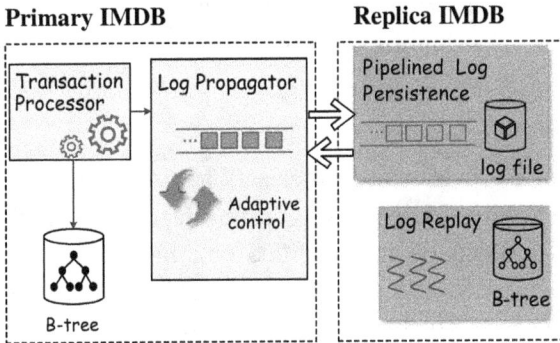

Figure 5.4: Overall architecture of QuorumX.

and replicates this log to all replicas. A transaction is committed by the primary when it receives the responses that more than half the followers have flushed the transactional log to non-volatile storage.

QuorumX includes two main modules, a replication processing module and a log replaying module. The replication processing module has two sub modules, one is the pipelined log persistence module in replicas, and the other is the adaptive control for log propagation in the primary. The pipelined log persistence is to speed up the log persistence process in a replica IMDB, and avoid the delay in processing logs in a completely sequential manner. The part of adaptive control in a primary is designed to consider the speed difference between the primary and replicas, and adaptively control the frequency of log propagation in a primary IMDB according to the processing speed of replicas to achieve the optimal performance under different environments. The log replaying module is responsible for the fast replay of received logs to memtables (which is often implemented by B+ Tree or SkipList in IMDB). Log replaying is designed to apply the replicated logs to memtables in a replica without coordination with the primary to reduce the risk of reading disks and minimize VGap on the premise of guaranteeing safety.

5.3 Replication Processing

Replication processing is to adaptively replicate the transactional logs to all replicas. In the following sections, we firstly introduce log format used in QuorumX, and then present pipelined log persistence mechanisms for reducing the replication latency. Finally, we explain how the adaptive log propagation algorithm is used by the primary IMDB.

5.3.1 *Log format*

After finishing the execution of transactional logics, the primary IMDB generates transactional logs, where the log records the modified data at the cell level (containing the modified column ID and its new value). QuorumX chooses value-logging for quick log replay, and reduces the network overhead by avoiding using the value-logging at the row level. The generated logs are filled into the buffer of log propagator at the primary. The *Log Entry* of QuorumX consists of the following fields:

- *Command_type*: Indicating the type of the log entry. There are two main types in QuorumX: update and non-update. The DML operations, such as *Update, Replace, Insert, Delete*, can be classified as update. The other operations, such as switching log file and checkpointing, are non-update operations.
- *Lsn*: Every log entry is uniquely identified by a log sequence number (Lsn). Lsns are ordered such that if Lsn_2 is greater than Lsn_1, the change described by the log entry with Lsn_2 occurred after the change described by the log entry with Lsn_1. The Lsn of a log entry is used as the version of replayed operations in a replica. The installed updates in a replica would be visible in order of their corresponding Lsns.
- *MaxComLSN*: The maximum Lsn of committed transactions in the primary is used to notify replicas to replay logs with Lsn smaller or equal to *MaxComLSN*.
- *Data*: Consisting of pairs of the modified cell/column ID and its new value. Note that the Lsn is installed together with cell modifications.

5.3.2 Pipelined log persistence

The basic steps for processing a received log by replicas are to parse and persist this log, and then send an acknowledgment to the primary IMDB. The replication latency of log processing is high if replicas use a dedicated thread to process received logs in a sequential manner. On the other hand, the received logs are required to be persisted according to

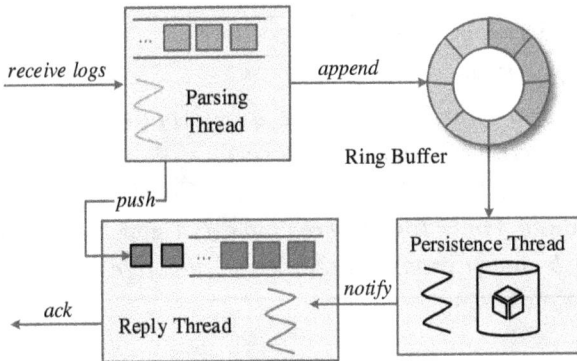

Figure 5.5: Pipelined log persistence scheme of QuorumX.

the order of their lsn. As a result, a simple parallelism strategy cannot work if replicas view each log as being independent, and process them completely in parallel. To reduce the time that a log takes to wait to be processed, QuorumX uses pipeline parallelism. The procedure of log persistence in a replica is partitioned into three stages: log parsing, log persisting and replying to primary. Figure 5.5. demonstrates the data flow in the pipelined log persistence. We omit the log replay phase from the pipeline and present the details of replaying logs in Section 5.4.

Algorithm 5.1 shows the main steps for parsing, persisting and reply threads. The parsing thread retrieves a package from the queue of network threads. The package is parsed to find the log entries, MaxComLSN and MaxRev_lsn (which denotes the maximal lsn received by a replica), at steps 4, 5 and 6. Log entries are appended to a *ring buffer* which is also shared by persisting and replaying threads. At step 8, the parsing thread pushes the package to a response queue which is shared with the reply thread. The persisting thread reads logs from the ring buffer (at step 3), flushes them to non-volatile storage (at step 4) and updates the persist_lsn (at step 5). The reply thread sends acknowledge to the primary if it finds the max_lsn of the head package of response queue is smaller than persist_lsn.

The replication latency is hidden through pipelined log processing. The parsing thread could process the next task even if the previous one has not been flushed. To reduce the IO cost of appending replicated logs

---

Algorithm 5.1: log persistence procedure

---

1 while *TRUE* do
2 | $package \leftarrow network\_thread\_queue.pop()$
        $log\_entries \leftarrow package.parse()$
        $MaxComLSN = log\_entries.MaxComLSN$
        $MaxRec\_lsn = log\_entries.max\_lsn$ append log_entry to
        $ring\_buffer$ $response\_queue$.push($package$)

---

1 while *TRUE* do
2 | $local\_buf = ring\_buffer.get(persist\_lsn,\qquad MaxRec\_lsn)$
        $flush(local\_buf)$ $persist\_lsn = MaxRec\_lsn$

---

1 while *TRUE* do
2 | $MaxRep\_lsn = response\_queue.head.lsn$ if
        $MaxRep\_lsn \leq persist\_lsn$ then
3 | | $response\_queue.pop()$ response to the primary

---

to files, the persistence thread aggressively persists a large batch of logs for each flushing operation. Similarly, once the persist lsn is found to be changed, the reply thread can pop many tasks at one time, and multiple logs are confirmed by sending only one response message to the primary.

Design choices for log buffer: The log buffer in a replica is responsible for caching the received logs from the primary. The persistence thread can flush a batch of buffered logs at one time, and the replay thread can directly apply the buffered log to keep up syncing with the primary. The design of log buffer needs to avoid reading logs from HDD or SDD for replaying logs. We choose the ring buffer as a FIFO data structure for transmitting data among the parsing, persisting and replay threads.

A key design consideration of a ring buffer is its size. If the ring buffer is set at a small size, the buffered and non-replayed logs would be covered by the new arrivals under heavy workload. Reading the covered logs from disk for replaying would introduce extra disk I/O latency. This causes the risk of cascading latency as more non-replayed logs continue to be covered by newly arrived logs. Finally, it will make the replica nodes never catch up with the primary. The basic principle of determining the buffer size is to satisfy *size* ≥ *generation_rate* ∗ *VGap*, where the *generation_rate* means the amount of logs generated by the primary in a second. We can estimate *generation_rate* by the performance characteristics of non-volatile storage. For example, in QuorumX, the primary uses an SSD with 500MB/s write speeds, therefore the *generation_rate* should not be greater than 500MB/s. If the VGap can be controlled within 1 second, the size of the ring buffer can be configured as 512MB. Some works optimized *generation_rate* by writing logs to multiple disks in parallel [93,104]. For example, SiloR could write logs at gigabytes-per-second rates. Caching all logs in the ring buffer leads to excessive memory consumption. We alleviate this problem by a coordination-free log replay (CLR) scheme presented in Section 5.4.

5.3.3 Adaptive log propagation

Under a heavy OLTP workload, the intuition of adaptive log propagation is that the count of transactional logs sent in a certain period of time cannot overload the capabilities of replicas. On the other hand, if the pipelined log persistence of replicas has an idle time slot, the performance of the IMDB cluster would be suboptimal. In QuorumX, the frequency to propagate logs is designed to match the processing capability of replicas. Batching is a general method to optimize the replication performance. Previous methods [51,85] often require the parameters (e.g., batch size) to be manually configured according to the degree of concurrency in workloads or network settings. QuorumX developed an adaptive log propagation scheme to dynamically tune send frequency to adapt to changing environments. Especially in highly concurrent workloads, QuorumX automatically adjusts the send frequency to avoid overloading replicas. In order to illustrate how to estimate the capability limit of

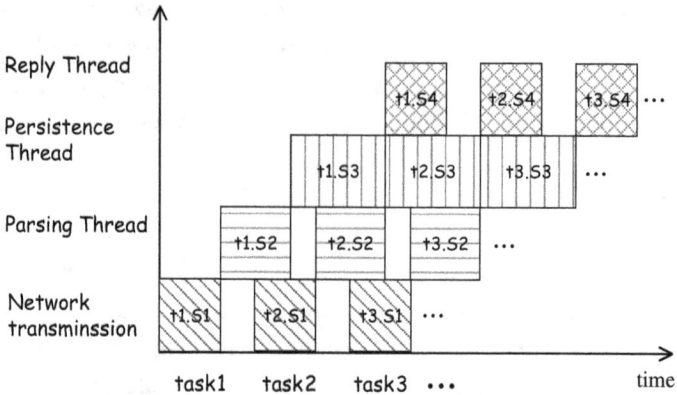

Figure 5.6: Pipelined execution of log replication.

replica nodes, we revisit the four phrases of the log propagation and persistence pipeline.

(1) Phase 1: The log propagator of the primary sends a batch of logs to replica nodes in a network package.

(2) Phase 2: The parse thread parses the received network packages into log entries, and appends them to the ring buffer.

(3) Phase 3: The persistence thread fetches logs from the ring buffer and persists them to disk.

(4) Phase 4: The reply thread sends a message to the primary to indicate that the logs have been replicated.

Figure 5.6 demonstrates how the four phases are executed in parallel. Phase 1 of the log propagation pipeline utilizes the network resource, and the number of transactional logs transmitted per second is limited to the network bandwidth and latency. Phases 2 to 4 are run on replica nodes. All operations in Phases 2 and 4 are executed in the in-memory and its performance should be bounded by the CPU. Phase 3 has disk I/O for each write operation and the capability of persistence thread is limited by the write speed of non-volatile storage media. In the pipeline parallelism, the number of instances concurrently running in the pipeline depends the most on the time-consuming phase. Phase 3 executed by the persistence thread is the slowest part for a replica node, and it determines

---

Algorithm 5.2: Adaptive Log propagation algorithm

---

1 $t_1 = response.parse()$ $queue.push(t_1)$
$sum = interval[replica]*(queue.size - 1)$ `if` $queue.size > SSW$
`then`

2 $\quad$ $tmp = queue.pop() - t_1$ $interval[replica]= (sum - tmp)/SSW$

3 `else`

4 $\quad$ $interval[replica]= (sum + t_1)/queue.size$

---

1 `forall` *replica* `do`

2 $\quad$ $current = system.getTime()$ $last = last\_send\_time[replica]$ `if`
$\quad$ $(current - last > interval[replica])$ `then`

3 $\quad\quad$ $start\_lsn = last\_send\_lsn[replica]$
$\quad\quad$ $inst = log\_buf.get(start\_lsn, max\_lsn)$ `send` $inst$ `to` *replica*
$\quad\quad$ $last\_send\_lsn[replica]= max\_lsn + 1$
$\quad\quad$ $last\_send\_time[replica]= current\_time$

---

the upper bound of processing capability. Thus, an optimal performance can be achieved when *the persistence thread handles tasks all the time and has no idle time.* We use the elapsed time spent on handling a batch (denoted as BatchTime) to denote the capability of a replica, and require the time interval of sending two batches not to be less than it.

Each replica monitors its BatchTime in the persistence thread, and sends it as feedback to the primary in reply messages. Primary calculates the interval of sending logs for each replica according to a sequence of BatchTimes in a fixed-size sliding window (*SSW*). As shown in the procedure *CALCULATE_INTERVAL* in Algorithm 5.2, the array *interval* stores the calculated intervals of each replica. When receiving reply messages from the reply thread in a replica, the primary parses the BatchTime of a handled batch and calculates the average interval in a *SSW*. In the procedure *SEND_LOG*, the primary sends a batch of logs to a replica when the time interval to the previous propagation is greater than *interval*[*replica*].

QuorumX can self-tune the interval of sending logs according to workloads or network configurations. When the influence factors of performance such as the number of concurrent clients, the characteristics of workload and network latency have no sudden changes, the interval of sending logs to a replica remains unchanged, and would be close to the BatchTime of this replica. We denote the send interval as t_x for a replica. Suppose that the number of concurrent increases dramatically. The size of a batch formed in t_x would become larger and the BatchTime of handling this batch would be longer than t_x. Thus, the updated *interval* array would have a new t_x which is greater than the old one for the replica. Then, the primary would decrease the sending frequency. Soon after, the send interval and the BatchTime of this replica reach the same value again. Similarly, when the network latency between the primary and replicas increases, the whole transaction latency would be longer. Thus, there are less logs in a batch if the send interval is still t_x. In this case, the persistence thread spends less time on processing a small batch. The BatchTime and the send interval would gradually reach the same smaller value.

5.4   Log Replay in QuorumX

A replica is required to replay the logs of committed transactions at a fast speed such that the data is kept fresh for real-time OLAP service. Additionally, a replica which has replayed all committed logs can immediately take over the failed primary and reduce the unavailable time of OLTP service. In this section, we present a parallel, CLR strategy for a replica with multi-version storage, and then analyze the advantages and problems introduced by this strategy.

5.4.1   Mechanism of coordination-free log replay

To guarantee data consistency, a replica is not allowed to replay received logs without commit notifications from the primary in the standard QR. These logs which wait for being committed and then are replayed should reside in the in-memory. However, limited ring buffer causes previously received and uncommitted logs to be erased by newly arrived logs. This introduces the extra disk I/O for log replay. CLR scheme is designed to reduce the residence time of received logs in a replica's in-memory. CLR makes a replica to directly apply the received logs to the memtable without waiting for the commit notifications. Obviously, CLR would hurt data consistency since the commit time of the same transaction on a replica may be earlier than that on the primary. For example, in an IMDB cluster with five machines, the primary sends the log of transaction T_x to the replicas. Since the network lost packets, only one replica R_1 received the log and replayed it immediately. At the same time, the primary has crashed. Since the log of T_x is not persisted to the majority machine, the transaction T_x decides to abort. It leads to R_1 being inconsistent with the newly elected primary IMDB. Therefore, QuorumX provides additional mechanisms to guarantee data consistency of CLR.

Log replay in CLR is divided into two phases. In the first phase, CLR uses multiple threads (referred to as replay workers) to replay logs for a replica. The second phase is to determine which version of the record is accessible. When an operation in a log is to modify a row, CLR firstly locks the row and installs the modification at the cell level into a linked list of this row. It should be noted that the lock on this row is released immediately after the operation is replayed. The installed updates are attached with lsn as its version number. Concurrent log replay may install the updates on a row with a different order from the primary. To guarantee the replica is prefix consistent with the primary, the second phase needs to make the installed updates be visible according to the order of lsn.

To clearly demonstrate CLR, we present an example in Figures 5.7 and 5.8. The SQL commands included in the *Transaction7*, *Transaction8*, and *Transaction9* are described in Figure 5.7. After completing the execution of transactions, the generated logs have lsn 7, 8, and 9, respectively, in Figure 5.8, referred to as log_7, log_8 and log_9. Replay worker threads (RW in the Figure 5.8) retrieve log_{7-9} from the ring buffer for replaying them in parallel. For each replayed log, RW pushes it into a global sorted list *g_list*. A publish thread advances the replica's *commit_lsn* in order to let updates from logs with lsn smaller than *commit_lsn* visible. The *commit_lsn* is refreshed to an lsn staying in *g_list* (referred to as *g_lsn*) which is not greater than the current MaxComLsn received from

```
Transaction₇ :
insert (col1, col2) values ('A', 1) into table1;
insert (col1, col2) values ('B', 1) into table1;
Transaction₈ :
update table1 set col2=col2*2 where col1= 'A';
update table1 set col2=col2+1 where col1= 'B';
Transaction₉ :
update table1 set col2=col2+1 where col1='A';
update table1 set col2=col2*2 where col1= 'B';
```

Figure 5.7: An example of transaction list executed in the primary.

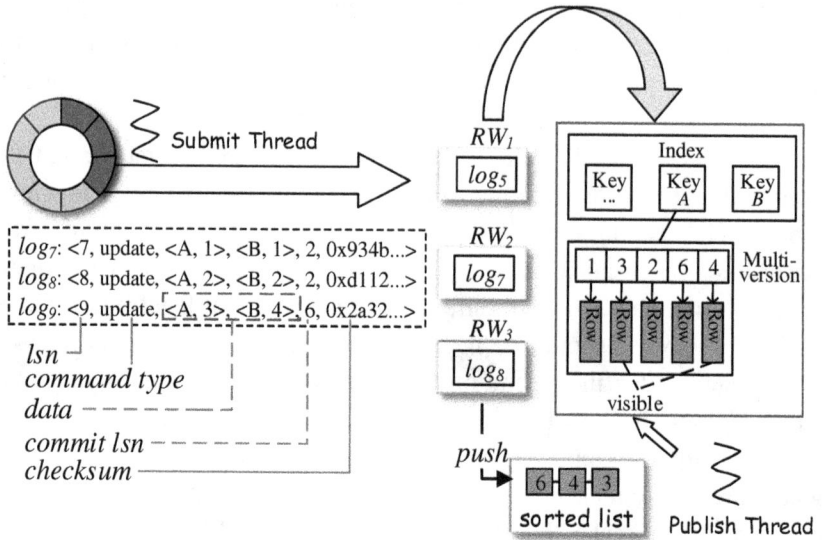

Figure 5.8: An example of replaying transactions in QuorumX.

the primary, and all logs with lsn from *commit_lsn* to *g_lsn* have been replayed. In Figure 5.8, the MaxComLsn carried by log₉ is 6. However, *g_lsn* should be updated from 2 to 4 because logs with lsn between 3 and 4 have been replayed. Therefore, the updates with version 3 and 4 can be visible. It should be noted that log₅ has not been replayed and not in the *g_list*, so the *g_lsn* can only be updated to 4 although the MaxComLsn is 6.

CLR immediately replays the received logs without waiting for MaxComLsn. One advantage is to avoid the risk of reading flushed logs from the disk. Besides, since CLR performs replay ahead of time, the VGap can be minimized compared with that in the classical quorum replay scheme.

5.4.2 Transaction rollback

The correctness of CLR depends on successful commits of replayed logs. When a replayed log has not been committed later by the primary, replicas which have replayed this log will revoke the uncommitted modifications to guarantee data consistency. Thanks to multi-version storage, a replica can easily find the uncommitted data for each row from a linked update with version numbers, i.e., lsn.

Various faults such as a crashed service process, outage or network partition are the reason that replicated logs fail to be committed by the primary. For example, in the case of network partition, an IMDB cluster consists of one primary and four replica nodes (i.e., the valid quorum size is three). Under the scenario where the network has been partitioned into two parts, one part contains the primary (i.e., $server_1$) and a replica node (i.e., $server_2$), and another part comprises the other three replicas (i.e., $server_3$, $server_4$ and $server_5$). As these two parts cannot communicate with each other, the quorum system will launch an election to elect a new primary (e.g., the new primary is $server_3$) in the partition with a majority of members. Before the occurrence of network partition, $server_1$ has only replicated log_5 to $server_2$, and other replicas have not received it. $Server_2$ has flushed log_5 to its disk and replayed it to memtable but not made it visible. However, the new primary, $server_3$, will generate another log_5 and send it to all replicas. $Server_2$ will receive and process two different logs with the same lsn when the network system is back to normal. In this case, QuorumX erases the old log_5 and rewrites the new one sent by $server_3$ to disk. However, with CLR, since log entry has been replayed to memory in $server_2$, re-replay the new log_5 will cause data inconsistency. The same thing will happen to $server_1$, the old primary. QuorumX supports transaction rollback mechanism, and $server_1$ and $server_2$ could revoke the modifications of uncommitted versions from memtables when the primary is switched because of various failures.

The locks of a transaction txn_1 are released immediately after its operations are replayed to memtables, but before txn_1 is committed. It means another transaction txn_2 could acquire the released locks even if txn_1 has not been committed. First, as QuorumX guarantees the modifications in replicas are visible according to the committed order from the primary, concurrent log replay has no inconsistent read problem. When the above-mentioned system failures occur, txn_1 should be rolled back. In this case, cascading rollback will happen. CLR revokes all uncommitted modifications from txn_1 and txn_1.

5.5 Evaluation

In this section, we evaluate the performance of QuorumX for answering the following questions through several sets of experiments. We use three benchmarks: a write-intensive micro-benchmark, a key-value workload (YCSB) [17] and an online transactional processing workload (TPC-C) [19].

- To reduce the commit latency, QuorumX uses pipelined log replication to accelerate the log processing of replicas. The first question is whether QuorumX shows higher throughput and lower transaction latency over the standard QR in highly concurrent OLTP workloads. In addition, we also want to know how much performance differences exist between QuorumX and the APR, although QuorumX is a replication scheme of guaranteeing strong consistency and the APR replication is that of sacrificing consistency for better performance (Section 5.5.2).
- QR needs to replicate transactional logs in a data center or cross data centers to tolerate various disasters. Another question is that whether QuorumX can adapt to different network settings. We also measure the adaptive capability of QuorumX under different degrees of concurrency in OLTP workloads (Section 5.5.3).
- The CLR scheme of QuorumX aims to reduce the VGap without waiting for commit messages and reading flushed logs for log replay. The final question is how QuorumX behaves under a continued, highly concurrent OLTP workload (Section 5.5.4).

5.5.1 System setup

We have implemented QuorumX in Solar [92] which is an open-source, scalable OLTP system originated from OceanBase with 437206 lines of code and developed by Alibaba. We added or modified 31282 lines of C++ code on the original code base which only supports APR. Therefore, Solar is a completely functional and high available IMDB system. A similar database system with QuorumX is also deployed in Bank of Communications, one of the biggest commercial banks in China.

Three replication methods are compared in the following experiments: the APR, standard QR and QuorumX, where the QR uses a single dedicated thread to handle logs without pipeline parallelism on the replica.

Cluster Deployment. The cluster in our experiments consists of 11 servers, and 3 servers are taken as IMDB nodes of Solar. The 3 IMDB nodes make a quorum, where one is the primary server and the other two are the replicas. The remaining 8 servers act as clients, receive requests and forward them to the primary. We increase the number of clients to result in an increase in concurrent transaction processing requests. Around 8 servers are able to support enough number of clients to reach the limit of transaction processing capacity of the primary IMDB. Each server is equipped with *two 2.3GHz 20-core E5-2640 processors, 504GB DRAM*, and connected by a *10 Gigabit Ethernet*.

Benchmarks. In the following experiments, we used two standard benchmarks and a micro-benchmark.

YCSB: The scheme of YCSB contains a single table (usertable) which has one primary key (INT64) and 9 columns (VARCHAR). The usertable is initialized to consist of 10 million records. A transaction in YCSB is simple and only includes one read/write operation. The record is accessed according to a uniform distribution.

TPC-C: We use a standard TPC-C workload with 45% NewOrder, 43% Payment, 4% OrderStatus, 4% Delivery and 4% StockLevel requests. We populated 200 warehouses in the database by default. The transaction parameters are generated according to the TPC-C specification.

Micro-benchmark: We build a write-intensive micro-benchmark. Instead of sending the primary IMDB transaction requests coded by SQL statement, this micro-benchmark directly issues raw write operations to the primary. Therefore, the primary IMDB is running under extremely high-concurrent, write-intensive workloads. By default, the micro-benchmark writes 10GB data modifications to the primary IMDB.

5.5.2 Transaction throughput and latency

YCSB. We measure transaction throughput and latency under a YCSB workload with full write transactions. The write-intensive workload can generate a large amount of transactional logs.

Experimental results of transaction throughput are shown in Figure 5.9. It is observed that QuorumX achieves the maximal throughput (135888 tps) when the number of concurrent connections is 100. The performance approaches to a stable state even when 120 client connections concurrently forward requests to QuorumX. QR reaches the maximal throughput (61711 tps) for 125 connections. Generally, the performance of QuorumX has an improvement of 2.2 × over QR. On the other hand, the primary IMDB using APR for replication does not have to wait for a majority of responses from replicas before committing transactions. Thus, APR can achieve the best throughput. However, QuorumX is optimized to hide the replication latency. Figure 5.9. shows that QuorumX has a similar throughput curve to APR. In the setting of write-intensive workloads, QuorumX only sacrifices 4% performance to provide data consistency and high availability.

Figure 5.10 presents the transaction latency with increase in the number of connections. Compared to QuorumX, QR spends more than 4 milliseconds when the number of connections is small. However, with the increase of connections, the QR's latency increases dramatically. This is because more and more received transactional logs to be processed are blocked in the task queue in the case of highly concurrent workloads. The latency of QuorumX has a similar trend to APR from the low concurrency of connection to high concurrency of connection. QuorumX only produces about 2 more milliseconds transaction latency caused by synchronous replication.

Different write/read ratios of YCSB. Figures 5.11 and 5.12 show the performance of QuorumX under YCSB workloads with different write/read ratios. We find that QuorumX always performs better than QR

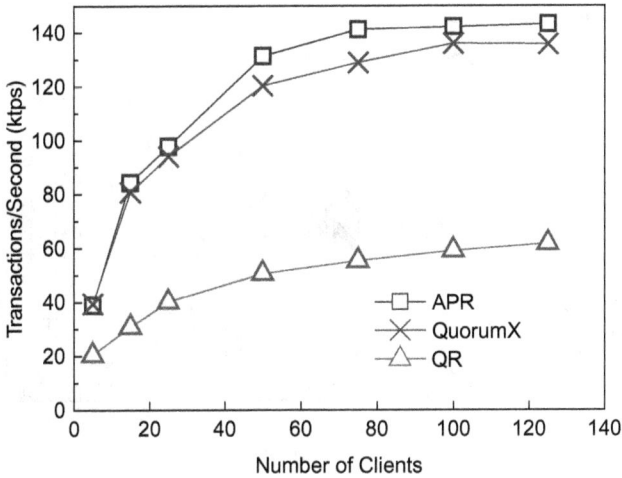

Figure 5.9: Transaction throughput under a write-intensive YCSB workload.

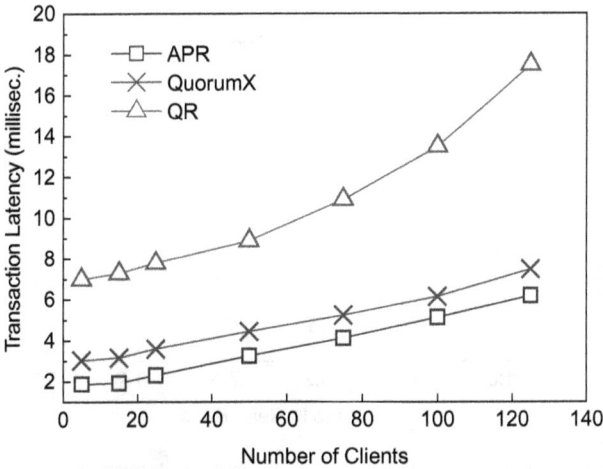

Figure 5.10: Transaction latency under a write-intensive YCSB workload.

with the increasing ratios of write to read. The throughput gap between QuorumX and APR is decreased from 4% to 1% as well as transaction latency from 2 to 0.5 milliseconds when workloads contain more read operations. This is because when the proportion of write operations decrease, the number of generated logs would also be decreased and

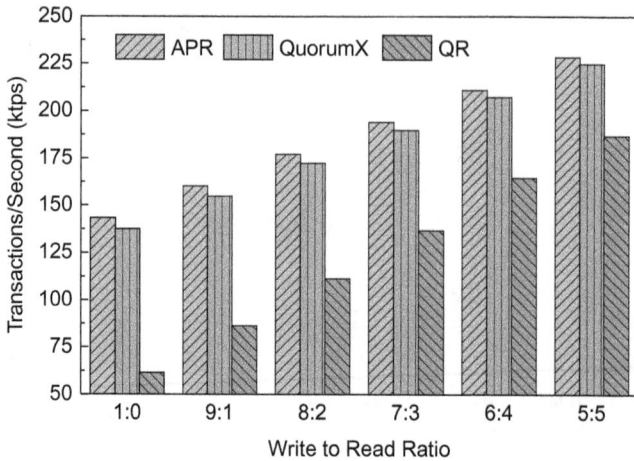

Figure 5.11: Transaction throughput under different write/read ratios in YCSB.

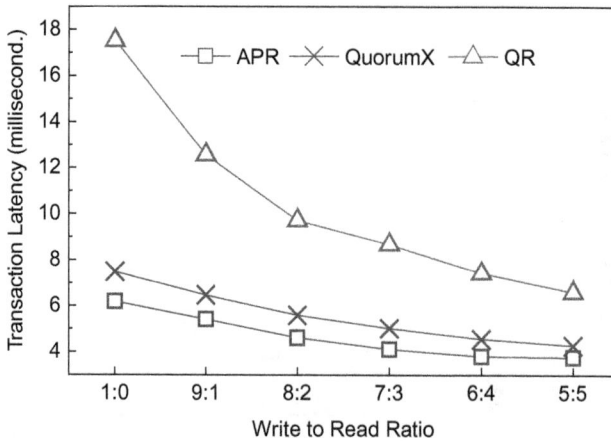

Figure 5.12: Transaction latency under different write/read ratios in YCSB.

then the impact of log replication on transaction throughput would have relatively reduced.

TPC-C. Figure 5.13. illustrates the throughput under a TPC-C workload by varying the number of connections. The number of warehouses is initialized to 200 in this experiment. We find that QuorumX has better performance than QR, and achieves a very close performance

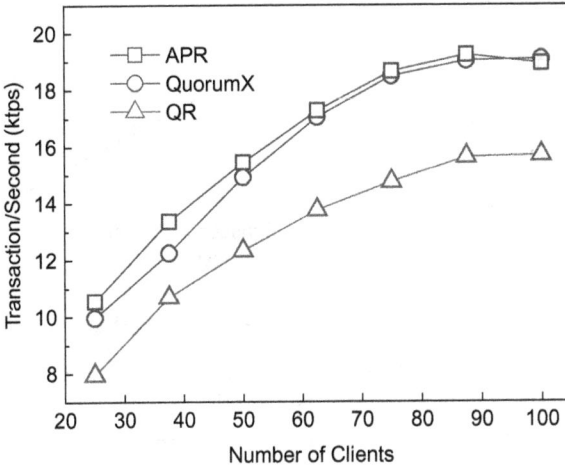

Figure 5.13: Transaction throughput under a TPC-C workload.

to APR. In addition, the throughput gap between QuorumX and APR in the TPC-C workload is smaller than that in YCSB. The reason is that a transaction in TPC-C contains more read/write operations than that in YCSB. When the primary IMDB is run under TPC-C, it takes more time on transaction execution and the cost of replication is relatively small. However, QR still suffers from high replication latency which results in a significant reduction in throughput. Results about transaction latency in TPC-C are omitted as the trend of latency is similar to that in YCSB.

5.5.3 Adaptivity of QuorumX

In this section, we evaluate whether QuorumX can adapt to various network environments and different degrees of concurrency in write-intensive workloads. QuorumX uses an adaptive control algorithm (referred to as ACA) to automatically tune batch size according to the feedback from replicas. Batching is a general method for optimizing the performance of replicating logs, and the batch size is fixed and needs to be adjusted manually for better performance.

Impact of Batch Size. We firstly demonstrate how the different batch size impacts transaction throughput under a YCSB-W workload with a fixed number of clients (125 clients). Figure 5.14 presents the throughput

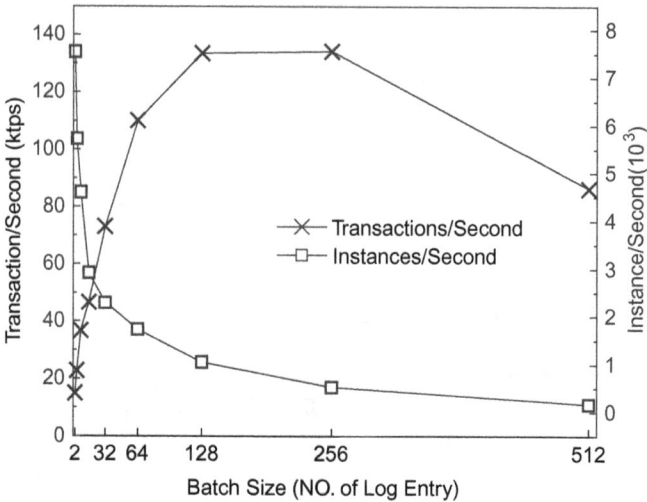

Figure 5.14: The relationship between performance and the batch size.

in different batch sizes. We find that both small and large batch sizes
can impair the performance. Obviously, the worst performance occurs
when the batch only contains a single log entry. The maximal throughput
in this experiment can reach 130k/s when the batch size is set to 256.
In this case, we find the replicas can process about 7,000 batches per
second. When the batch size is far beyond 256, the throughput decreases
because the transactional logs take more time to construct a big-size
batch in the primary IMDB, and the log processing pipelines in replicas
might be idle. The goal of ACA is to adaptively find the most suitable
batch size in dynamic environments.

Adaption for Network. Rigorous testing of a network device or
distributed service requires complex, realistic network test environments.
Linux Traffic Control (tc) [23] with Network Emulation (netem) provides
building blocks to create an impairment node that simulates such networks.
Using the netem *qdisc*, we can emulate different network latency and
jitter configurations on all outgoing packets. We monitored the transaction
throughput in the primary IMDB, and the network configuration is
changed two times during monitoring. Network configurations include
0.2, 5 and 20 milliseconds, which corresponds to the Local Area Network
(LAN), Metropolitan Area Network (MAN) and Wide Area Network

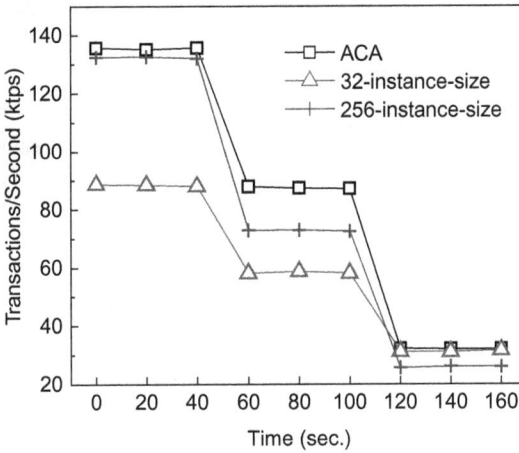

Figure 5.15: Performance under different networks.

(WAN), respectively. The initial network latency is 0.2 milliseconds. We modified it to 5 milliseconds after 40 seconds, and changed it to 20 milliseconds 100 seconds later. We monitor the throughput of ACA and the traditional batching method with two fixed sizes: 32 and 256. Experimental results are shown in Figure 5.15. When the network latency is 0.2 milliseconds, we find that there is little performance difference between ACA and the batching with fixed 256 log entries. The fixed batching size with 32 cannot perform well. However, when the network latency is changed to 20 milliseconds, ACA and batching with size of 32 have similar performance, where the batching with size 256 has the worst performance. This is because when the network has a large latency, the primary should increase the send frequency such that more batches arrive at the log processing pipeline of a replica in time. It should be noted that the batch size is decreased with the increasing send frequency when the number of clients is fixed and each client forwards the request after it receives the response of the previous request.

Adaption for High Concurrency. We evaluate the adaptivity of QuorumX by varying the number of clients from 5 to 125. The performance of QuorumX is presented in Figure 5.16. It is observed that when the number of clients is small, ACA and 32-instance-size have a close performance. But in the high client-concurrency, ACA and

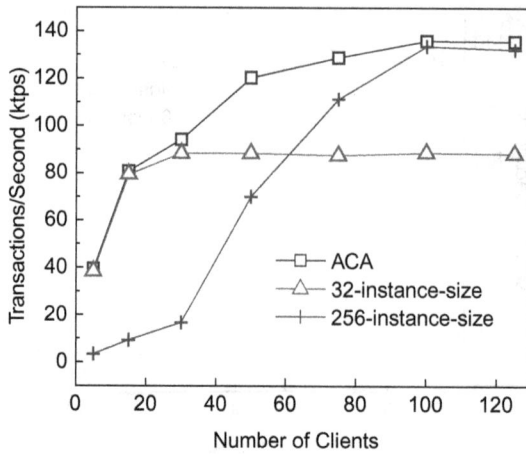

Figure 5.16: Performance under different client-concurrency.

256-instance-size have a better performance. This suggests that ACA can automatically tune its batch size and adapt to different concurrency. In the setting of 125 clients, we measured the average value of interval array in ACA for a replica, and it was about 2 milliseconds. According to the throughput i.e., 130k/s, we can calculate that the average size of a batch formed in 2 milliseconds is 260, where $batch\_size = tps * send\_interval$, i.e., $(1.3 * 10^5) * (2 * 10^{-3})$. Thus, the realtime batch size used by ACA is very close to 256, which is a fixed batch size for performing well in 125 clients.

5.5.4 VGap of log replay scheme

We measure the VGap between the primary and replicas to explore the effect of our safe and coordinate-free replay scheme under a continued, highly concurrent and write-intensive micro-benchmark. The VGap is the time difference between a transaction being committed in the primary and its data being visible in a replica. In this experiment, the local clocks of the primary and replicas were synchronized by Network Time Protocol (NTP). The VGap of QuorumX with CLR, QuorumX without CLR, and APR is presented in Figure 5.17.

Figure 5.17 demonstrates that the VGap of QuorumX without CLR keeps growing and finally increases sharply over time. By analyzing trace

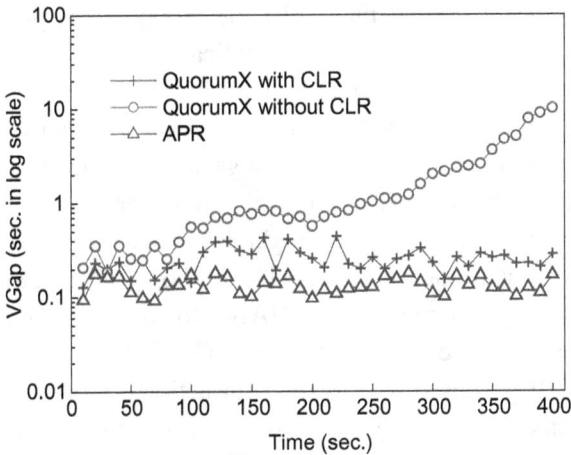

Figure 5.17: The effect of CLR on VGap.

logs, we found that more received and committed logs are evicted from in-memory because of the limited log buffer. The replicas performed disk-read operations for getting flushed logs to replay, which causes synchronous I/O delay. QuorumX with CLR has a stable VGap, and most of it is under 0.5 seconds since CLR avoids disk-read. The APR can achieve a best VGap because replicas can replay logs, and later the committed data are visible immediately.

5.6 Related Work

Replication is an important research topic across database and distributed system communities [47,97]. In this section, we review relevant works mainly on two widely used replication schemes, i.e., primary-backup replication and QR.

Primary-Backup Replication. APR [88], proposed by Michael Stonebraker in 1979, has been implemented in many traditional database systems. In most typical deployment scenarios, APR is used to transfer recovery logs from a master database to a standby database. The standby database is usually set up for fault tolerance, and not required to provide the query on the latest data. The performance of log replication and replay have not received much attention in the last several decades. Recently, researchers [36,58] suggest that serial log replay in the primary-backup replication can cause the state of the replica server being far behind the primary with modern hardware and under heavy workloads. KuaFu [36] constructs a dependency graph based on tracking write-write dependency in transactional logs, and it enables logs to be replayed concurrently. The dependency tracking method works well for traditional databases under normal workloads, and it might introduce overheads for IMDB under highly concurrent workloads. The author of Ref. [58] proposed a parallel log replay scheme for SAP HANA to speed up log replay in the scenario where logs are replicated from an OLTP node to an OLAP node. Qin *et al.* [80] proposed to add the transactional write-set into its log in SQL statement formats. This method can reduce the logging traffics, and replicas can concurrently execute SQL statements in replicated logs with write set.

Log replay in classical QR has different logics to APR. Replicas using QR cannot replay received logs to memtable immediately like the primary-backup replication, and they need to wait for MaxComLSN from the primary. Due to this difference, these works that optimize log replay for primary-backup replication cannot directly apply to the QR.

Despite the low transaction latency, the APR cannot guarantee high availability and causes data loss when the primary is crashed. PacificA [60] resolves these problems by requiring the primary to commit transactions only after receiving persistence responses from all replicas. The introduced synchronous replication latency depends on the slowest server in all replicas. Kafka [16] reduces replication latency by maintaining a set of in-sync replicas (ISR) in the primary. Here, ISR indicates the set of replicas that keep the same states with the primary. A write request is committed until all replicas in ISR reply. Kafka uses the high watermark (HW) to mark the offset of the last committed logs. The replicas in ISR need to keep the same HW with the primary. When the offset of a replica is less than HW, it would be removed from ISR. Through ISR, Kafka can reduce negative impact on performance caused by the network dithering.

Quorum-based Replication. Replication based on consensus protocols is referred to as QR, which is also called as state machine replication in the community of distributed system. Paxos-based replication ensures all replicas to execute operations in their state machines with the same order [15]. Paxos variants such as Multi-Paxos used by Spanner are designed to improve the performance. Raft [73] is a consensus algorithm proposed in recent years. One of its design goals is more understandable than Paxos. For this reason, Raft separates log replication from the consensus protocol. Many systems such as AliSQL[a] and etcd[b] adopt Raft to provide high availability. However, these systems use Paxos or Raft to replicate meta data, where replication performance is not a serious problem. Spanner as a geo-distributed database system supports distributed transactions, and each partitioned database node is not designed to handle highly concurrent OLTP workloads. AliSQL only uses Raft to elect leader in the occurrence of system failures. Etcd is a distributed, reliable key-value store that uses the Raft for log replication. Similar to Zookeeper [38], these kinds of data store are designed to provide high availability for meta data management and are not suitable for highly concurrent OLTP workloads.

There are a few works on tuning replication performance of Paxos with batching and pipeline [51,85]. Nuno Santos and Schiper [85] built an analytical model to determine the batch size and the pipeline size through gathering a lot of parameters like the network latency, bandwidth and the application properties. The author of Ref. [51] proposed to generate batches and instances according to three parameters: the maximum number of instances that can be executed in parallel, the maximum batch size, and the batch timeout. These parameters need to be set manually and cannot adapt to various environments.

5.7 Conclusion

In this chapter, we address the problems of quorum-based data replication for IMDB under highly concurrent workloads. We propose a pipelined log replication scheme and an ACA to solve the speed mismatch between the primary and replicas. Received logs in a replica can be processed by QuorumX without blocking, and thus commit latency of transactions

---

[a] AliSQL. https://github.com/alibaba/AliSQL.
[b] etcd website. https://coreos.com/etcd/.

is reduced. Further, a safe and coordinate-free log replay mechanism is designed to replay logs immediately without depending on its committed notifications. It avoids the risk of replaying logs from disk, and also reduces the VGap between the primary and replicas.

Experimental results show that QuorumX achieves a great improvement in straightforward implementation of QR. Compared with the APR, QuorumX only sacrifices 3–8% performance to support strong data consistency and high availability.

6

Follower Recovery

6.1 Introduction

Faced with the failures of cheap commodity machines, modern data store systems often employ replication techniques to increase fault tolerance and scalability. According to Brewer's CAP theorem [9, 28], a data store providing strongly Consistent services cannot maintain highly availability property in the presence of complete network Partitions. Therefore, one main challenge of using replication is how to trade off the three properties. Replication techniques can be classified into two categories according to whether they are based on distributed consensus protocol or not. Many popular NoSQL systems, like Amazon's Dynamo [22] and Facebook's Cassandra[a], adopt replication based on non-consensus protocol and they can provide horizontally scalable and highly available services even if the network is partitioned, but they sacrifice the consistency. In recent years, the state machine replication (SMR) based on Paxos consensus protocol has received much attention from both industry and academia as it can guarantee strong consistent services and provide robust failure models.

However, the basic version of Paxos is well known for its difficulty of understanding. Many details of implementation have not been described in the original Paxos papers. This leads to existing systems adopting Paxos

---

[a]Cassandra website. http://cassandra.apache.org/.

protocol, such as Spanner and Chubby, possibly having implemented an unproven Paxos variant [10, 15]. Therefore, in order to enhance the understandability and facilitate implementation, some multi-Paxos variants using *strong leadership* and *log coherency* features—which ensure that a log entry must be consistent with the leader's and there are no holes in the log—are proposed. Raft [73] is the most typical one of them and it has been used in many open source data stores or database systems, e.g., CockroachDB[b], etcd (see footnote b of chapter 5) and TiDB.[c]

In the Raft replicated system, the log of a replica may be inconsistent with that of another node due to the fact that a replica can persist a log entry regardless of whether the corresponding write is committed. We analyze the log inconsistency anomaly in Section 6.3.1. Therefore, to guarantee the correctness and consistency of the system, when a replica recovers as a Follower, it needs to handle its local log carefully. The conventional follower recovery methods (the details is presented in Section 6.3.2) usually need many network round trips or more data to be transferred, and thus result in increased follower recovery time.

In this chapter, we present the **F**ollower **R**ecovery using **S**pecial mark log entry (**FRS**) algorithm, which does not depend on *commit point* strongly and requires only one network round trip for fetching the minimum log entries from the leader when a follower is recovering. The following is the list of our main contributions:

- We give the notion of the special mark log entry, which is the delimiter at the start of a term.
- We introduce the **FRS** algorithm, explain why this mechanism works and analyze it together with other approaches.
- We have implemented the **FRS** algorithm in the open source database system OceanBase (see footnote a of chapter 4). The performance analysis demonstrates the effectiveness of our method in terms of recovery time.

---

[b]CockroachDB website. https://www.cockroachlabs.com/.
[c]TiDB website. https://github.com/pingcap/tidb.

This chapter is organized as follows. First, preliminary works about log replication model based on Raft are presented in Section 6.2. We introduce the special mark log entry and how the leader uses it to take over in Section 6.4. Section 6.5 describes the FRS algorithm, whose correctness is also proved and performance is analyzed. In Section 6.6, we introduce the implementation of FRS in a real database system. Section 6.7 presents the performance evaluation. The related works are described in Section 6.8. We conclude this chapter in Section 6.9.

6.2 Preliminaries

In this section, we introduce the log replication model adopting the *strong leadership* and *log coherency* features, which is based on Raft, but has some difference from the original. Also, we give the properties of this replication using formalization.

- Strong leader: The leader replica is responsible for all the write requests, and it is the only one that can generate log entries.
- Log coherency: There are no holes in the persisted log of each replica.

Although checkpoint and snapshot are the other important aspects of recovery technique in the database literature, this work focuses on the replica recovery based on log replication. Our proposed method is easy to extend for the recovery setting with checkpoint or snapshot.

6.2.1 The overview of Raft replication

To provide highly available services, the replicated database systems are usually deployed on a cluster of collaborative commodity machines, where each one is a replica node used as a state machine and mapped to one of the three roles: *Leader*, *Follower* or *Candidate*. Traditionally, systems adopting Raft protocol have two main phases: *leader election* and *log replication*, whose executions can be overlapped. For ease of description, we assume that each replica node is a main-memory database system and the total number of state machines is N.

In these replicated systems, time can be divided into consecutive terms of arbitrary length, with each one being numbered with a monotonically

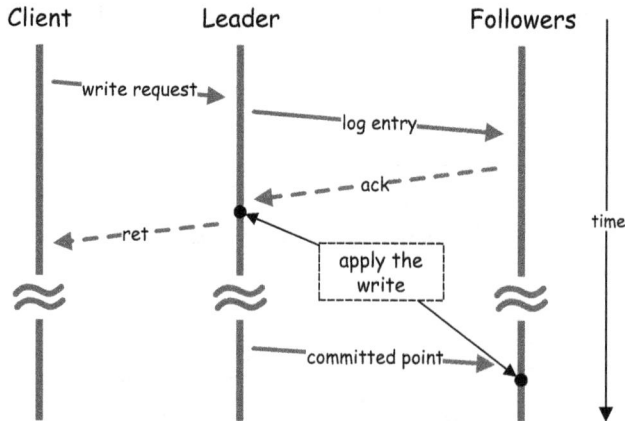

Figure 6.1:   The Raft replication model: the solid lines and the dashed lines represent requests and responses, respectively.

increasing integer $term\_id$. In each term, there is one and only one leader which is responsible for log replication.

During normal processing of log replication, only the leader of a term can accept the write requests from clients. Figure 6.1 shows the model of log replication in the Raft replicated system. When receiving a write, the leader generates a log record which contains the monotonically increasing log sequence number (LSN), its own $term\_id$ and updated data. Next, the leader replicates the log entry to all follower replicas. When the entry is persisted on a majority of nodes, the leader can apply the write to the local state machine and send a reply to the client. Then the leader updates the local committed LSN, which is called *commit point* (*cmt*) and can be piggybacked by the next log message. All the replicas are assured that the writes in a log entry with LSN less than *cmt* are applied. Therefore, the followers storing consecutive log entries can only apply the committed writes to local state machine in the order of log sequence.

Note that the leader always makes a write visible first, which is illustrated by the black spot in Figure 6.1. If a client wants to read the latest data, the simplest way is to issue the request to the leader. Although this processing scheme can satisfy the strongly consistent read, it sacrifices the scalable performance as only the leader can handle read requests. Another method is the leader forwards the read request to followers. However, the read request can be blocked at the follower to wait the latest data/logs being applied.

The leader sends a heartbeat to all follower replicas periodically in order to maintain its authority. If a follower assumes that there is no leader in the system, it becomes a candidate and increases the current *term_id*, and then launches a leader election. According to the last log entry, a new leader with the highest *term_id* and LSN can provide services only when it receives a majority of votes.

6.2.2 The properties of Raft replication

For ease of description, we now briefly formalize the concept of log and give the properties of Raft replication.

Let L_j denote a log entry where j is the LSN, and let $\log(i, j)$ represent the sequence of log entries $(L_i, L_{i+1}, \ldots, L_j)$. For brevity, $\log(j)$ is used to replace $\log(1, j)$ where 1 is the LSN of the first log entry. And we use the notation $L_i.par$ to access its parameter that is named *par* (e.g., $L_i.term\_id$ is the term value recorded in L_i).

Definition 6.1 (Committed Log Entry). If a log entry L_i has been persisted on a majority of replica nodes, it is a committed log entry.

To distinguish the logs in different replica nodes, we use L_i^s to denote the log entry L_i stored on the replica node s. Similarly, we use $\log(i, j)_s$ to represent the log sequence $\log(i, j)$ on the node s.

Definition 6.2 (Log Entry Equivalence). Let s and t denote different replica nodes. If $L_i^s.term\_id = L_j^t.term\_id$ and $i = j$, then $L_i^s = L_j^t$.

If $L_k^s = L_k^t$ for $k \in \{i, i+1, \ldots, j\}$, we use $\log(i, j)_s = \log(i, j)_t$ to denote it. If $L_j^s.term\_id \neq L_j^t.term\_id$, then L_j^s is not equal to L_j^t, which is represented by $L_j^s \neq L_j^t$.

Definition 6.2 is the same as the first Log Matching Property described in Raft [73], which follows from the fact that a leader generates at most one log entry with a given LSN in a given term, and a log entry never changes its position in the log.

Theorem 6.1. *Let ℓ and f denote the leader and a follower. If f knows that its L_i^f is a committed log entry, then $L_i^f = L_i^\ell$.*

Proof. Since L_i^f is a committed log entry, then the term of L_i^f is the same in at least a majority of replica nodes containing the leader ℓ according to the majority rule of election. In other words, $L_i^s.term = L_i^\ell.term$. Therefore, $L_i^f = L_i^\ell$.   □

6.3 Problem Analysis

In this section, we present an analysis about the log inconsistency anomaly incurred by failure recovery in the Raft replicated system and summarize the methods used in existing systems to resolve this problem.

6.3.1 Log inconsistency anomaly

In the Raft replicated system, a log entry is not committed until it is persisted by a majority of replicas. In other words, a replica node can write a log entry into the local disk regardless of whether the entry is received by other replicas. Therefore, there may exist non-committed log entries in the non-volatile storage of a replica. This may lead to an anomaly that the log of a replica is not consistent with the Leader's if the leader role is transfered.

Figure 6.2 shows an example of log inconsistency anomaly in a 3-replica system. R1 is the leader at that moment, and R3 which used to be the leader fails and stops. Because only R3 flushed the log entries 5

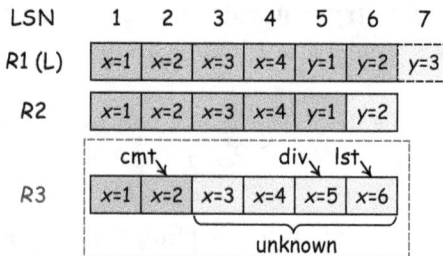

Figure 6.2: An example of log state of 3-replica at a time point. R1 is the leader and R3 failed. According to the local *cmt* (*commit point*), a replica can ensure that the log entries represented by the boxes with dark gray are committed.

and 6 before it failed, $\log(5, 6)_{R3}$ which is different from $\log(5, 6)_{R1}$ is the invalid log. Recall from Section 6.2.1 that the *cmt* (*commit point*) is an LSN used to indicate the log before this point can be applied to local state machine safely, which is persistent in local. The *div* (*divergent point*) is the LSN of the first one of the log entries which are invalid in the order of log sequence. The *lst* (*last point*) is the LSN of the last one of a log. Note that the *cmt*, *div* and *lst* of R3 are 2, 5 and 6, respectively.

To ensure that a replica's state is consistent with the leader's, the replica node has to make sure that its log is identical to the leader's when it recovers as a follower. Therefore, it needs to find the non-committed log entries in the local log and discard the invalid log, where each is not equivalent to the committed one with the same log index. Then it gets the missing entries and applies the committed ones in the log order. In Figure 6.2, when R3 restarts as a follower, it needs to replace $\log(5, 6)_{R3}$ with $\log(5, 6)_{R1}$ and apply the committed log entries from 1 to 6. We give a more formal definition of follower recovery as follows:

Definition 6.3 (Follower Recovery). Given a recovering follower f and its local *last point* $f.lst$. The recovery of f succeeds only if f discards all invalid log entries, gets and persists all missing committed log entries not larger than $f.lst$ from the leader replica, and replays all these entries.

A recovering follower has to handle the local unknown log entries correctly. Unfortunately, R3 in Figure 6.2 does not know the state of the log after the *cmt* (LSN 2). In other words, the follower cannot locate the *div* directly. In the next subsection, we will describe the typical solutions to avoid the negative effects caused by log inconsistency anomaly.

6.3.2 Typical solutions

Recall that a replica node flushed a log entry to local storage first. Then the log entries, whose LSNs are not larger than *cmt*, can be safely applied to the local state machine. However, the state of the log after *cmt* is unknown. In other words, a log entry whose LSN is greater than *cmt* may be committed or invalid.

Fortunately, a recovering follower f can get the *cmt* from local—which is denoted by $f.cmt$—and be assured that the log entries whose LSN is not larger than this point are committed. Next, it needs to handle the local log after $f.cmt$ carefully. There are two ways to handle the log entries in unknown state:

- **Checking (CHK):** The recovering follower f gets the log entry $L_{f.lst+1}^{\ell}$ from the leader ℓ, and then it checks whether $L_{f.lst+1}^{\ell}$ is continuous with $L_{f.lst}^{f}$. If not, it will discard the log entry $L_{f.lst}^{f}$, decrease $f.lst$ by 1 and repeat the above process; otherwise, it will get the missing committed log entries from the leader by one request.
- **Truncating (TC):** The recovering follower f gets the log$(f.cmt + 1, \ell.lst)$ from the leader ℓ. Then it truncates the local log after $f.cmt$ and appends the received log to local, all of these operations should be done atomically. More precisely, the received log$(f.cmt + 1, \ell.lst)_{\ell}$ can be flushed in local, and then log$(f.cmt + 1, \ell.lst)_{f}$ can be truncated. Finally the received log is appended to local.

It is clear that the CHK is simple and the TC is complicated, because the replacement operation of TC can be interrupted and more steps are required to handle each exceptions, e.g., if a recovering follower fails again and the appending operation is not finished, it has to do the appending when it restarts. Both of approaches cannot locate the div directly, which leads to more network round trips or more transmitted log entries in the follower recovery. We will propose a new approach in the next sections, which needs only one network round trip for getting the minimum number of log entries.

6.4   The Special Mark Log Entry

In order to reduce the overhead of follower recovery, we must provide an additional mechanism which can record necessary information used in the recovery of a follower. In this section, we introduce the special mark log entry and the way a new leader utilizes the special entry to take over the write requests from the clients.

6.4.1   Overview

A special mark log entry S is the delimiter at the start of a term. Let S_i and S denote the special mark log entry of the term i and the set of all

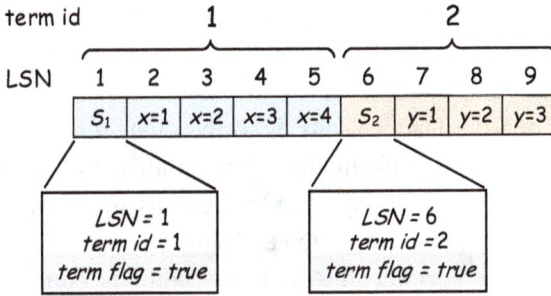

Figure 6.3: An example of log with special mark log entry. Log entries represented by the boxes with the same color belongs to one term. Because of two terms existing in history, there are two special mark log entries S_1 and S_2 in the log.

existing special entries, respectively. Also, we use the notation $S_i.par$ to access its parameter named *par* (e.g., $S_i.lsn$ represents its LSN). In order to distinguish the other log entries from the special ones, we call them the normal operation log entries, which are the members of the set $\mathcal{N}$.

To establish a special mark log entry, a mark flag should be embedded in each log entry. An S, differing from the normal operation log entries, does not contain any updated data, and its mark flag is set to *true*. Figure 6.3 shows an example of the log including the special mark log entries. The boxes which are filled with the color of the same gray level are the log entries belonging to the same term. Therefore, we cannote that L_1 and L_6 are the special mark log entries for the term 1 and 2, respectively, i.e., S_1 and S_2.

6.4.2 Leader takeover

The notion of the special mark log entry has been introduced. Note that only the leader can produce the S and generate only one for its term. We now describe how the special entry is generated and used when a new leader enters into takeover phase.

When a replica is elected as a new leader, a new term gets started. To guarantee that the local log entries from the previous term are committed, the new leader must take some actions before it provides the clients with normal services. Therefore, the leader using special mark log entry can perform the following steps to take over:

(1) According to the new term id t, the leader generates the special mark log entry S_t. More specifically, it produces a log record with a greater LSN and the term id t, and sets the *mark_flag* of the entry to true. Then the leader sends S_t to the other replicas.

(2) The leader gets the information of committed LSN *commit_point* from local log, and replays the log records up to this point in the background. It gets the followers' information and refreshes the *commit_point* periodically until this point is equal to or greater than the LSN of S_t. Note that the leader cannot service the requests from the clients in this phase.

(3) The leader can safely apply the whole local log entries to the local state machine (e.g., the memory table). Then it can provide the clients with the normal services.

Algorithm 6.1 shows the pseudocode of the function `Server_as_leader`, which contains the three steps described above. It is clear that the function can only be called by a new leader when it wins the election.

Theorem 6.2. *L_i is the last log entry of a log and $L_i.term\_id = t$. If L_i is not a special log entry, then S_t is committed.*

Proof. Assuming that $S_t.lsn = j$. Since the LSN is monotonically increasing and $i \geq j + 1$, we can confirm that L_{j+1} is produced. According to the leader takeover using the special mark log entry, the $L_{j+1} \notin S$ is generated and replicated only when the leader ensures that the S_t resides on a majority of the replicas. Therefore, we can conclude that S_t is a committed log entry. □

6.5   Fast Follower Recovery

In this section, we will describe the FRS, prove its correctness and make an analysis on its network overhead. For ease of description, we assume that the recovering follower only needs to handle log entries not greater than the local *last point*.

Algorithm 6.1: Leader takeover algorithm

---

1 <u>Function</u> `serve_as_leader`(*new_term*)
| /* phase 1   */
2 | generate a log entry s;
3 | $s.term\_id = new\_term$;
4 | $s.mark\_flag = true$;
5 | send s to other replica nodes;
   | /* phase 2   */
6 | get *commit_point* from local storage;
7 | start threads to replay log entries to the *commit_point*;
8 | `while` *commit_point* < *s.lsn* `do`
9 | | sleep for a while;
10 | | get followers' information and refresh the *commit_point*;
11 | `end`
   | /* phase 3   */
12 | apply the whole log entries;
13 | provide normal service;
14 `end`

6.5.1 The FRS algorithm

When a replica node recovers from a crash and finds that its role is a follower, it should take some measures to ensure that its own state is consistent with that of the leader. More precisely, the recovering follower has to discard the invalid log entries in local storage and get the committed ones from the leader. Then it can apply the writes in the log to local state, so that the follower can reach a consistent state with the leader. The recovering follower can leverage the special mark log entries to reduce the cost of recovery. The procedure is drawn by `recover_as_follower` function in Algorithm 6.2. The main steps are as follows:

(1) The recovering follower gets the *commit_point* and *last_point* from the local storage first. Then it obtains the last committed special log

---

Algorithm 6.2: FRS algorithm

---

1 <u>Function</u> recover_as_follower()
2   get *commit_point* and *last_point* from local storage;
3   get last committed special mark log entry *s* from local log;
4     $start = \max(commit\_point, s.lsn)$;
5     $end = last\_point$;
6     $result = \text{confirm}(start, end)$;
7   if $result \neq 0$ then
8   remove the entries from the local log after $result - 1$;
9   get $LOG(result, end)$ from the leader;
10   append $LOG(result, end)$ to the local log;
11   end
12   replay log entries and provide normal services;
13 end
    /* Function confirm is a RPC which is executed
       in the leader   */
14 <u>Function</u> confirm(*start, end*)
15     $result = 0$;
16   for $i = start + 1$ to *end* do
17   if $L_i.mark\_flag == true$ then
18           $result = L_i.lsn$;
19   break;
20   end
21   end
22   return *result*;
23 end

---

entry s (i.e., there exists a log entry l where $l \in \mathcal{N}$ and $l.lsn > s.lsn$). We set two variables *start* and *end* to $\max(commit\_point, s.lsn)$ and *last_point*, respectively. Note that the *start* indicates the LSN of the last committed log entry, which can be figured out by the recovering follower itself. After that, the follower calls the confirm function—whose pseudocode is show in Algorithm 6.2—with *start* and *end* as input parameters, which is a remote procedure call (RPC) and needs to be executed in the leader replica.

(2) When the leader receives the request of executing `confirm` function from the follower, it gets the input parameters *start* and *end* first. Then the leader scans the local log from *start* to *end*, and obtains the first special log entry *s* in this range. If no one satisfies the requirement, the leader will reply with a result value *zero* to the follower; otherwise, it will return the LSN of *s*.

(3) When the follower receives the response of the `confirm` function, it checks the result value v. If v is not *zero*, the follower will first discard the entries with LSN greater than $(v - 1)$ from the local log. Next, it gets all committed log entries in the log range (v, end) from the leader and appends them to the local log. If v is *zero*, the follower will not copy with the local log.

When a follower replica recovers from a failure, it first calls the function `recover_as_follower` to eliminate invalid log entries in the local storage and acquire the consecutive ones from the leader. Next, the follower can replay the local log safely. Then it processes the log replication using the normal approaches described in Section 6.2.1.

The **FRS** algorithm is applied not only to the restarting from a failure but also to the scenario where a follower finds that a new leader is elected. Generally, if the term is changed, the lease of previous leader is expired, and the follower will turn to candidate and then convert to follower again when it knows that the new leader is not itself. In this case, the follower invokes the `recover_as_follower` function actively. There is another case that a follower receives a special mark log entry or a log entry containing a newer term value. In this scenario, the follower dose not change its role, and it only discards the buffered log and then executes the **FRS** algorithm.

6.5.2 Correctness

Now we show why the **FRS** algorithm works. Specifically, we should explain whether the result returned by the `confirm` function is correct. If the returned value v of `confirm` function is *zero*, then the log entries stored in the recovering follower will be consistent with that of the leader; otherwise, the v will be the *divergent point*.

Let ℓ and f represent the leader and the recovering follower, respectively. To prove the correctness, we use the following two lemmas.

Lemma 6.1. *If the returned value of* `confirm` *function is zero, then* $\log(end)_f = \log(end)_\ell$ *where end is the LSN of the last log entry in* f.

Proof. The input parameters of `confirm` function are *start* and *end*, which can be abbreviated to s and e, respectively. In the worst case, the $f.cmt$ is *zero*, which indicates that the information of $f.cmt$ is damaged. According to Theorem 6.2, L_s^f is a committed log entry. Therefore, we can refer to Theorem 6.1 and conclude that $\log(s)_f = \log(s)_\ell$.

Assuming that $L_s^f.term\_id = t$, we can note that $L_s^f.term\_id = L_s^l.term\_id = t$. Since the returned value of `confirm` function—which is set to *zero* initially—is *zero*, there does not exist any special mark log entries in $\log(s+1, e)_l$. And $\log(s+1, e)_f$ does not contain any special entries, we can learn that $L_i^f.term\_id = L_i^l.term\_id = t$ for $i = s+1, s+2, \ldots, e$. Therefore, $\log(s+1, e)_f = \log(s+1, e)_l$. In combination with $\log(s)_f = \log(s)_l$, we can get the conclusion that $\log(e)_f = \log(e)_l$. □

Lemma 6.2. *If the returned value of* `confirm` *function is* v *and* v *is not zero, then* $\log(v-1)_f = \log(v-1)_l$ *and* $L_i^f \neq L_i^l$ *for* $i = v, v+1, \ldots, end$.

Proof. We reuse the notations described in the proof of Lemma 6.1. Since there are no special mark log entries in $\log(s, v-1)_f$ and $\log(s, v-1)_l$, according to the proof of Lemma 6.1, we can conclude that $\log(v-1)_f = \log(v-1)_l$. Since the returned value of `confirm` function is v and v is not zero, L_v^l is a special mark log entry. Because the *term_id* is monotonically increasing, we can know that $L_i^l.term\_id \geq t+1$, which is not equal to $L_i^f.term\_id$ for $i = v, v+1, \ldots, e$. Therefore, we can conclude that $L_i^f \neq L_i^l$ for $i = v, v+1, \ldots, end$. □

According to Lemma 6.1 and Lemma 6.2, we can conclude that the FRS algorithm can guarantee the correctness of data.

6.5.3 Analysis

For ease of understanding, the FRS algorithm described above may need two requests to the leader, one for confirming the local log and another for acquiring the log entries. Fortunately, we can merge the requirements of the two requests into the `confirm` function. More precisely, when the leader receives the `confirm` request, if it finds a special mark log entry s in the log range $(start, end,$ then it will return the local log entries after $(s.lsn - 1)$ directly; otherwise, it will return *null*. If the recovering follower gets the result *null* from `confirm` function, it will replay all local log and change to the normal state; otherwise, it will get the first log entry f from the result and replace the local log after $(f.lsn - 1)$ with the result.

According to the optimization described above, the FRS algorithm needs only one network round trip. And we know the number of transmitting log entries in the FRS is minimal from the above sections. Table 6.1 shows the comparison of the FRS and other follower recovery approaches, which contains the number of log entries and round trips needed in the recovery, in the case that the log(cmt, lst) in the recovering follower is repaired to be consistent with leader's.

Note that the results in Table 6.1 do not consider the cost of the special mark log entries. This is because the size of a special entry is fixed and small (less than 100 bytes). For example, assuming that the size of each write is 100 bytes, if a term includes only 100 normal operation log entries, the size of the corresponding special one accounts for less than 0.5% of the total log size of the term. Therefore, the cost

Table 6.1: Comparison of different approaches of follower recovery. It should be noted that *lst* and *cmt* represent *last point* and *commit point* of the recovering follower's log, and *div* denotes the LSN of the first divergent log entry between the follower and leader.

Approach	log entries	Round trips
CHK	$2 \times (lst - div + 1)$	$lst - div + 2$
TC	$lst - cmt$	1
FRS	$lst - div + 1$	1

of the special mark log entries can be ignored in the normal case. In the next section, we will propose a set of techniques in our implementation, which can improve the system performance and accelerates the follower recovery.

6.6 Implementation and Optimization

In this section, we describe the implementation of **FRS** algorithm in the open source database system OceanBase 0.4.2, which is a scalable open source RDBMS developed by Alibaba. It consists of four modules: management server (RootServer), update server (UpdateServer), baseline data server (ChunkServer) and data merge server (MergeServer). Note that an UpdateServer is a main memory database with original key-value structure, which is used as a state machine in Raft replication, and the RootServer is responsible for leader election.

Recall from Sections 6.2.1 and 6.4 that the synchronization of a log entry is triggered by each write request from a client, which can produce massive disk and network IO operations. Therefore, in order to reduce the replication overhead, the UpdateServer adopts *batching* mechanism to synchronize a batch of log entries each time. When the leader generates a log record for a write request, it inserts the entry into a log buffer, which is a queue in the leader replica. If the size of log entries in the buffer reaches the maximum capacity or the time interval of two consecutive batches exceeds a predefined value, the leader packages the buffered log entries and sends them to the followers by an asynchronous method. Besides, the leader flushes these replicated log entries to local disk.

To guarantee the correctness of Theorem 6.2, the first batch of a new leader can only contain the special mark log entry s of the new term. When the leader fills s into the log buffer successfully, it replicates the log entry immediately. When a follower finds out that the first log entry f of a batch is the special one ($f \in S$), it realizes that a new leader is elected. Then it checks whether f is the next one for the local log. If it is, the follower will append s to the local log file safely and return an acknowledgment; otherwise, the follower will invoke the recover_as_follower function to recover the local log.

When a follower receives a set of log entries from the leader, it caches these entries into the log buffer firstly. Then, the follower checks the buffered log entries to guarantee that there do not exist holes in the log sequence and their LSNs are continuous with persistent log in local storage. Finally, the buffered log entries can be appended to the log file. Otherwise, the follower gets the missing ones—which are regarded as a group if they are continuous—from the leader.

The *batching* mechanism can reduce the overhead of disk and network effectively. In practice, there exist many factors impacting the follower's recovery time. Therefore, we have to consider these influences and optimize the implementation to accelerate the follower recovery.

6.6.1 Tuning in leader

In FRS algorithm, the leader has to locate the *divergent point* for the recovering follower. Although the lookup cost may be decreased with the help of the whole log range (*start, end*) provided by the follower, the leader still needs to scan the log to get this point in local disk such that the recovery time of the follower is increased. In our implementation, we adopt a set of techniques to reduce the overhead of the leader for follower recovery.

Quickly Locating the Divergent Point: Recall from Section 6.4 that the new leader has to generate and synchronize a special log entry when it is taking over. The receiving log entry of a replica needs to be appended to the local log file directly, and the naive implementation leads to the size of log file is increasingly larger. Since reading a file always starts from the header, a large log file is not suitable for locating the *divergent point*. Therefore, when the term is changed, each replica needs to generate a new log file for the new term and to add the special log entry to the new file, which is named log.term_id.lsn where the lsn and term_id is the information of the first log entry in the log file. The newly generated log entries need to be appended to this file. An example is illustrated in Figure 6.4. The log filenames indicate that there are two special log entries S_1 and S_2, and $S_1.lsn$ and $S_2.lsn$ are 1 and 6, respectively.

Caching Special Log Entries: Each replica has to cache all special log entries' information into its memory when it is replaying local log. When the leader receives the confirm request, it only traverses S in the order of terms and gets S_i that is the first one whose LSN is in

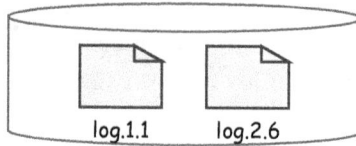

Figure 6.4: An example of log files in a replica. The file name contains the term and LSN information.

the range $(start, end)$, i.e., the divergent point. Then we read log files whose terms are greater than i and transfer the committed log entries to the recovering follower. Note that this mechanism avoids reading the log entries whose LSNs are less than the divergent point from the file.

Only Flushing Data: The Unix system called fsync needs to flush the metadata of a file, which increases the disk activities. Therefore, to improve the performance of flushing transactional log entries, the conventional database system utilizes the function fdatasync—which does not flush the metadata—instead of fsync. More specifically, a log file is initialized with a fixed size and a name containing an integer identifier, and new log entries are appended to it by using fdatasync. If the file is full, a new log file is created with an monotonically increasing identifier.

6.6.2 Tuning in follower

If recovering from a crashed state, a follower has to take two steps to guarantee the correctness of its state machine: catch up with the leader and replay log. In the catching up phase, the recovering follower retrieves the missing log entries from the leader. In the replaying phase, the follower replays the committed log entries to build the local state machine. To ensure that its state is consistent with the Leader's, the two steps are executed serially, i.e., the follower can take the catch-up step first and then perform to replay log.

Recall from Section 6.2.1 that a follower persists the received log entries and replays the log when it is acknowledged that the leader has committed them. The process of log persistence and log replaying can be executed in parallel. When a follower receives log entries from the leader, it updates its local commit point firstly, then pushes the log entries to a log buffer and finally writes them to the disk in a single thread. On the other hand, a group of replay threads waits for log replaying. When the commit point is updated, the replay threads get log entries from the log buffer and replay them in parallel. The replayed log entries are pushed to a single commit thread in the log sequence order to ensure that the commit order is the same as that of the leader.

6.7 Performance Evaluation

In this section, we evaluate different follower recovery schemes including the proposed FRS algorithm and other traditional methods.

6.7.1 Experimental setup

Cluster platform: We ran the experiments on a cluster of 12 machines, and each machine is equipped with a 2-socket Intel Xeon E5606 @2.13GHz (a total of 8 physical cores), 96GB RAM and 100GB SSD while running CentOS version 6.5. All machines are connected by a gigabit Ethernet switch.

Database deployment: The Raft group (RootServer and UpdateServer as a member) is configured with 3-way replication and each of them is deployed on a singe machine in the cluster. Each pair of MergeServer and ChunkServer is deployed on one of the other 9 servers.

Competitors: We compare the FRS algorithm to other approaches described in Section 6.3.2. The CHK approach is responsible for locating the *divergent point*. To find the divergent log index, the recovering follower requires the leader to send all log entries after div. Therefore, the number of requests of CHK is half of the results described in Section 6.5.3. The follower adopting the TC approach gets the log after cmt which is contained by one message package from the leader.

Benchmark: We adopt YCSB [17]—a popular key-value benchmark from Yahoo—to evaluate our implementation. In order to generate enough transactional log entries, we modify the workload to have a read/write ratio of 0/100. The size of each write operation is about 100 bytes. The client applications, which issue the write requests to the database system, are deployed on the MergeServer/ChunkServer nodes.

6.7.2   Experimental results

To measure the performance of follower recovery, we need to kill a replica node and then restart it. Therefore, each experimental case is conducted as follows. First, we insert about one million records to the system. During this phase, we execute the leader election several times. Next, we make the in-service leader r disconnect from the other replicas before its lease expires. This leads to the invalid log entries generated in r. When r loses the leadership and a new leader is elected, we kill and restart r. Then r recovers as a follower.

Network overhead

We first measure the statistics of the follower recovery in terms of received requests in the leader and received log entries in the recovering follower. Therefore, we get the results by adding codes to cumulate the corresponding values in the program.

Figure 6.5 shows the statistics of a recovering follower, which fails in different workloads denoted by different numbers of clients. As the number of clients increases, we find that the sizes of $log(cmt, lst)$ and $log(div, lst)$ become larger, which can lead to more requests and received log entries in the follower recovery. Figure 6.5(a) shows that CHK approach needs hundreds of requests to locate the div point, and the other approaches need only a few network interactions in the

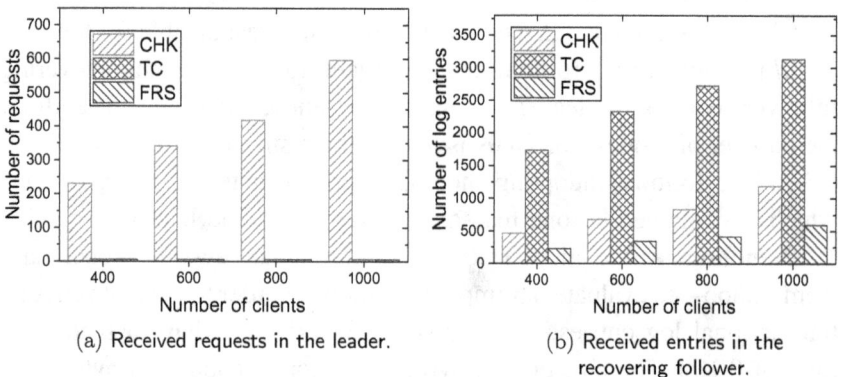

(a) Received requests in the leader.

(b) Received entries in the recovering follower.

Figure 6.5: The statistics of a recovering follower which used to be a leader and fails in different workloads.

recovery phase. Figure 6.5(b) shows that the TC transmits the most log entries containing the unnecessary ones. Since the log transmitted in locating *div* is not preserved, the number of logs received are about twice the FRS's. All of these results conform to the analysis described in Section 6.5.3.

Recovery time

Note that the recovery of a follower has two phases: handling log in unknown state and applying the log to local machine state, which are also called *log recovery* and *state recovery*, respectively. In order to observe different methods clearly, we first measure the time of handing the uncertain log entries. In this experiment, the recovering follower fails when the number of clients (workload) is 400.

Figure 6.6 shows the log recovery time with valid *commitpoint* when the system is in different workloads and with different network delays. We use Linux tool tc to add the network delay of the recovering follower. As the number of clients increases in Figure 6.6(a), we find that the log recovery time of TC and FRS is not changed obviously, and the results of the two approaches are close to each other. The reason is that the size of $LOG(cmt + 1, div - 1)$ does not consume bandwidth excessively. The result of CHK method is linearly correlated with the number of clients, which indicates that the higher workload can lead to more time of handling a request in the Leader. The trend in Figure 6.6(b)

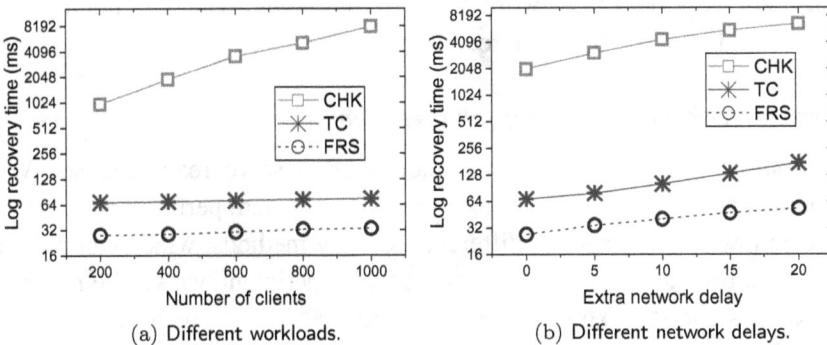

(a) Different workloads.   (b) Different network delays.

Figure 6.6: Log recovery time when *cmt* is valid.

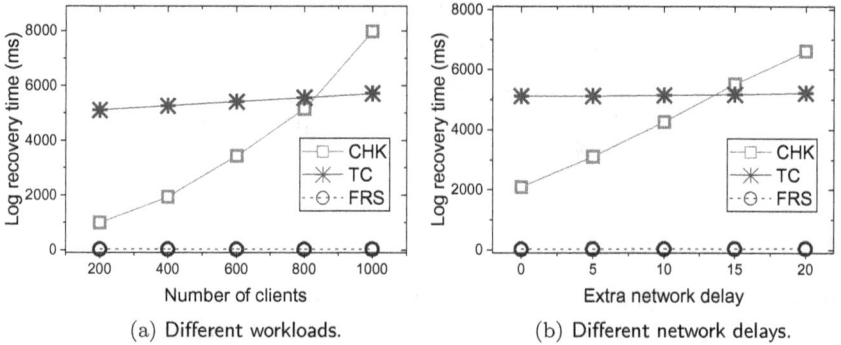

(a) Different workloads.   (b) Different network delays.

Figure 6.7: Log recovery time when *cmt* is invalid.

is similar to Figure 6.6(a). Accordingly, high workload or high network delay has a negative impact on the recovery time of the CHK.

Note that *cmt* may be not updated in append mode, a valid *cmt* may not be available when a node restarts as a Follower. Figure 6.7 shows the log recovery time with invalid *cmt*. Since CHK and FRS do not completely depend on the *cmt* information, we find that the results of the two approaches are similar to those in Figure 6.6. However, if the *cmt* is invalid, a recovering follower adopting TC needs to get the all log entries from the leader. Due to the long time of transforming the total log, the recovery time of TC—which is between 5s and 6s—is not desired. Accordingly, the *cmt* information has a significant impact on TC for the recovery time.

Therefore, FRS works better in terms of log recovery time under different workloads or network delay. Furthermore, FRS does not depend on a valid *cmt* for follower recovery.

System performance during follower recovery

In real application, the follower nodes often serve read requests. We conduct an experiment to evaluate the overall system performance during the follower recover using different recovery methods, which can reflect the total time of follower recovery. In this experiment, we set the number of clients and the extra network delay to 1000 and 0, respectively.

Figure 6.8 shows that the change of throughput over time. We kill the leader and restart it at 10 and 15 seconds, respectively. When we

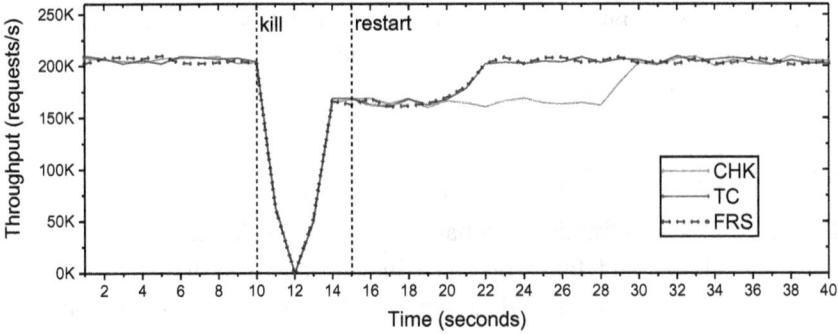

(a) Valid cmt.

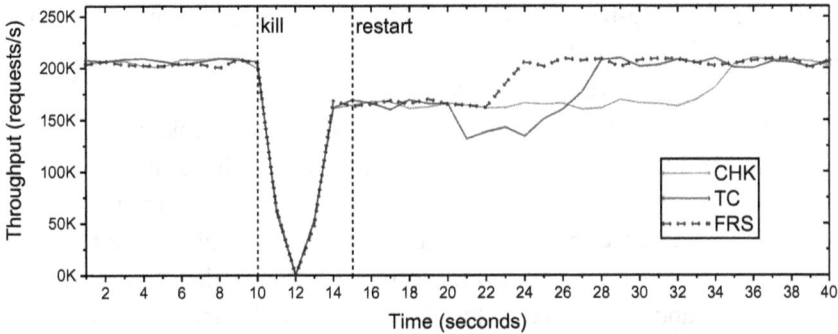

(b) Invalid cmt.

Figure 6.8: Impact on clients' requests: the number of clients and the extra network delay are 1000 and 0, respectively.

kill the leader, the results of throughput drop to zero until the new elected leader took over the requests from the clients. Due to the loss of a replica's capacity after killing the replica, the performance could only return to four-fifth that of faultless system. When we restart the non-running replica, if the *commit point* is valid, TC and FRS will take approximately the same length of time to return to the normal of 3-way replication, and CHK will take more time. These results are illustrated in Figure 6.8(a), which confirms our analysis in the previous section. Figure 6.8(b) shows the results when the *commit point* is invalid. Owing to the properties of the special mark log entry, the line of FRS is similar to that in Figure 6.8(a). The recovering time of CHK becomes longer, because it cannot replay the log entries until the log recovery finishes.

Since TC has to pull the whole log from the leader replica, not only does it take more time to recover, but also the overall throughput is impacted due to the use of the leader's network bandwidth.

6.8 Related Work

Replication is an effective mechanism to provide horizontal scalability, high availability and fault tolerance in distributed systems. SMR [86], a fundamental approach to designing fault-tolerant services, can ensure that the replicas are consistent with each other only if the operations are executed in the same order on all replicas. In reality, database systems utilize log-based recovery [11] and lazy master–slave replication mechanism [30] to realize SMR.

Paxos, which was first described by Lamport in Ref. [57] and simplified in Ref. [58], is a protocol for SMR in unreliable environment. Modern distributed database systems deployed on a cluster of commodity machines often use Paxos protocol to achieve highly available services without sacrificing consistency. Chubby [10] is a fault-tolerant system based on Paxos at Google, which offers a reliable distributed locking mechanism and file system to Google's core business. Google has developed MegaStore [3] and Spanner, which utilized Paxos for log replication, to provide highly available and consistent database services. Although these systems are published in papers and running successfully, their implementation details are not clear.

Using Paxos to implement a highly available system is non-trivial. Chandra *et al.* [15] describe some algorithmic and engineering challenges encountered in moving Paxos from theory to practice and give the corresponding solutions. To further increase understandability and practicability, some multi-Paxos variants adopting strong leadership are proposed. In Spinnaker [82], the replication protocol is based on this idea. Nevertheless, its leader election relies an external coordination service ZooKeeper[d] [38]. Raft [73] is a consensus algorithm designed for educational purposes and ease of implementation, which is adopted in many open source database systems, e.g., CockroachDB (see footnote b)

---

[d]ZooKeeper website. http://zookeeper.apache.org/.

and TiDB (see footnote c). Although these protocols can guarantee the correctness of follower recovery, they neglect to locate the *divergent point* directly.

There are many other consensus algorithms which are similar to multi-Paxos. The Viewstamped Replication (VR) protocol [72] is a technique that handles failures in which nodes crash. ZooKeeper Atomic Broadcast (Zab) is a replication protocol used for the ZooKeeper (see footnote d) configuration service, which is an Apache open source software implemented in Java [44]. Renesse *et al.* [95] presented the differences and the similarities between Paxos, VR and Zab. In the following subsections, we describe the typical systems and protocols, and analyze their follower recovery.

6.8.1 ZooKeeper

ZooKeeper, an open source implementation based on the Google's lock service Chubby, is a project of the Apache Software Foundation, which can be used as a fault-tolerant distributed coordination service to build a highly available distributed application. It can be regarded as a small replicated database system consisting of a configurable number of replica servers, one leader and multiple followers, each one a full copy of a hierarchical key-value store.

Zab protocol, a crash-recovery algorithm, is a critical component of the system. It is responsible for the correctness of the state machine of any replica in any case. A follower leverages the property of ZooKeeper transaction id (zxid) to recover from a crashed state. The zxid, a 64-bit number, has two parts: a 32-bit epoch and a 32-bit counter. When recovering, the follower first connects to the Leader and sends a registration with the zxid of the local last log entry l. Then the leader checks the zxid and synchronizes the follower with the committed log entries whose epochs are greater than the value of l's zxid. Note that the first one of the synchronized log may be the *divergent point*.

The follower recovery algorithm is similar to our method, which can locate the *div* and minimize the number of log entries transmitted. However, it has some shortcomings: (1) The leader blocks the write requests during the Follower recovery, since the log is locked when the leader synchronizes the recovering follower. This can reduce the availability of write service. (2) The leader traverses the local log—which may persist in the disk—to find the *div*. Therefore, the leader may visit many unnecessary log entries whose zxids are less than or equal to the recovering follower's last log entry's. This increases the disk IO and the time of follower recovery.

6.8.2 Raft

Raft is a distributed consensus algorithm which produces a result equivalent to Paxos, but Raft is more understandable and easy to implement in practical systems. Raft ensures that the replicated log in each state machine is in the same order and it can be used in many large-scale systems which have a single leader.

In raft replication, only leader accepts new request from clients, replicates log entries to followers, and decides when it is safe to apply log entries to their state machines. While receiving a request command from a client, the leader appends it to a local log file and replicates by broadcasting AppendEntries RPC to each follower. The leader updates its commit index and applies the command to local state machine when the majority of followers accepted it. Finally, the leader broadcasts the commit index in the next AppendEntries RPC. Once the follower learns that a log entry is committed, it commits and applies the entry and other previous entries.

In Raft, the log entries are only transferred from the leader to followers and the leader's log can't be deleted. The inconsistent log on a follower will be diagnosed by AppendEntries consistency check. While a machine is recovering from a crash, it starts checking the uncommitted log entries one by one to reach a point where the logs of the leader and follower match each other. The inconsistent log entries after this point will be replaced by the committed ones from the leader. Accordingly, the recovering follower finds the *divergent point* using CHK to compare more log entries, this leads to consuming more time on network round trips. Raft optimizes this by checking and bypassing all of the conflicting entries of one term but still needs many network round trips to reach an agreement.

To reduce the commit latency of transaction log from the previous term, the leader of the current term can generate a no-op log entry and commit this entry [37]. The idea of creating a no-op log entry at the beginning of a new term is similar to our special log entry method. However, the goal of this work is to use the special log to enable an efficient follower recovery.

6.8.3 Viewstamped replication

VR is a replication protocol proposed during the same era with Paxos [72], and the authors introduced a updated version in the 2012 [62]. In the case of normal operations, the primary replica is responsible to order the write requests and then forward them to backup replicas. A backup replica will handle the received request only if the previous requests have been processed. The request is committed when the majority of members have received it. When the primary failed, VR used a consensus protocol similar to Paxos to choose the new primary. The replicated operations/logs are flushed to disk by the background thread, and checkpoints are periodically carried out. When a backup replica failed, its recovery first needs to load the latest checkpoint from local disk or other normal replicas, and then the recovering replica retrieves the suffix log entries from other replicas after the checkpoints. As the execution of VR didn't require the disk IO for the *commit point*, it denotes that the latest committed request is not persisted to non-volatile storage. Therefore, the failed replica cannot use *cmt* information to accelerate the recovery procedure.

6.8.4 Spinnaker

Spinnaker, developed by IBM, is an experimental key-value data store that is designed to run on a large cluster of commodity servers in a single datacenter. It uses horizontal partitioning to divide the rows of a table into disjoint key ranges, with each one replicated to N servers ($N = 3$ by default). Each group of nodes involved in replicating a key range is denoted as a *cohort*.

Spinnaker relies on a distributed coordination service ZooKeeper for leader election. It adopts the truncation method to guarantee that the state of a recovering follower is consistent with the leader's, and it persists the *commit point* in each replica. More precisely, when recovering, the follower first re-applies the committed log entries whose LSNs are less than the local *cmt*. Then it obtains the committed log after the *cmt* from the leader, and replaces the local log after the *cmt* by logical truncation.

Owing to adopting the truncation method, Spinnaker reduces the number of network round trips in the follower recovery. However, more log entries need to be transmitted, especially when the information about the committed entries is missing or corrupted.

6.9 Conclusion

Fast follower recovery is a non-trivial problem in Raft replicated systems. The recovery procedure not only needs to guarantee the correctness of data, but also bring the recovering replica back to normal as fast as possible. In this work, we introduced an efficient FRS. It does not require the storage of persistent commit point and can transmit the least number of log entries by using only one network round trip. The experimental results demonstrate the effectiveness of our method in terms of recovery time.

7

Summary and Future Trends

7.1 Summary

Commodity servers are generally equipped with big DRAM and multi-cores, and these machines have been widely deployed in data centers. Recently released database systems can take advantage of big memory to hold the entire working dataset into memory for high-performance transaction processing. Main memory database systems have removed most performance bottlenecks in traditional disk-based DBMS such as slow DISK I/O, buffer pool management and locking overhead incurred by centralized lock managers. However, new bottlenecks appear in other components of main memory databases such as in-memory storage engine and concurrency control for high-performance OLTP. Furthermore, modern OLTP applications have new requirements on database systems in addition to transaction processing performance. Two main requirements include the scalability and high availability of the system.

In this book, we first presented EMS, an efficient MVCC storage engine, to optimize the read/write performance by co-locating the latest two versions. EMS is able to reduce the overhead of point chasing which decreases the read/write performance of existing MVCC storage engines. We also proposed an efficient concurrency control for workloads mixing OLTP and bulk processing. By tracking the conflicts on the granularity of logical ranges, our method can filter out unrelated transactions and reduce the cost of validation phase in OCC. Replication is the key technique to support the scalability and availability for distributed main memory database systems. We have designed and implemented an efficient global snapshot isolation scheme based on Paxos replication. The follower can handle read requests under the guarantee of strong snapshot semantic similar to traditional centralized database. Furthermore, we propose an adaptive log replication to prevent the follower from being overloaded by considering the capability of follower nodes. Finally, the availability of the system is optimized by designing a fast follower recovery mechanism.

7.2 Future Trends

Scheduling on Operations. To improve the performance for high-contention workloads, modern main memory database systems (e.g., Calvin or H-store) usually assume that all operations in a transaction are known in advance, and thus generate a conflict-free schedule. However, due to the scalability and flexibility of the Multi-Tier architecture, in many OLTP applications, instead of using stored procedure, their business logics are still implemented by using interactive JDBC/ODBC-like API. In this scenario, a transaction is executed in an interactive manner, referred to as interactive transaction. Most database systems use a queue to buffer transaction operations sent from different clients, and employ the FIFO strategy to handle each operation. It leads to the result that interactive transactions are executed in a non-predetermined order, and high-conflict transactions easily block each other or are frequently aborted. Therefore, it is promising to schedule operations for interactive transactions under high-contention workloads.

Based on the assumption that transaction logics are implemented by stored procedure, Calvin is able to generate conflict-free schedule. Calvin yields deterministic execution order according to the read and write sets of transactions before their executions. The intelligent scheduling proposed in Ref. [107] scheduled conflicting transactions into the same queue. Under one-shot transaction model, it first predicted all read/write set of a incoming transaction. Then, the conflict possibility is measured by comparing read/write sets with those running transactions in each queue. All the above scheduling works avoid executing two conflicting transactions concurrently. However, in the case of interactive transactions, we cannot decide whether one transaction conflicts with another before its execution. Therefore, existing transaction scheduling methods are not suitable in the context of interactive transactions.

Adaptive Concurrency Control. Recently, a kind of emerging application (e.g., online fraud detection or finance risk analysis) has demands for real-time analyses on transactional data. A transaction in these applications may mix OLTP-style operations and analytic queries, known as hybrid transactional and analytical processing (HTAP) [50,74]. Lightweight concurrency control protocols mainly optimize conflict detection at the row level and lack efficient mechanisms to guarantee a serializable schedule for HTAP transactions. Under heterogeneous workloads, the cost introduced by concurrency control schemes has a significant impact on overall performances, and it has received surprisingly little attention.

All the mixed concurrency control protocols are mainly concentrated on exploiting the benefits of pessimistic method under high-conflict workloads and optimistic mechanism under low-conflict workloads [6,12,90,91]. However, even under heterogeneous workloads with low contentions, validation schemes used by an OCC protocol have a significant impact on the performance. Under heterogeneous workloads, the cost introduced by concurrency control schemes has a significant impact on overall performances, and it has received surprisingly little attention. Conflict detection methods should be adaptively selected according to the type of an operation in a transaction and the characteristics of its current workloads.

Bibliography

[1] A. Ailamaki, R. Johnson, I. Pandis, and P. Tözün. Toward scalable transaction processing: Evolution of shore-mt. *VLDB*, pp. 1192–1193, 2013.

[2] P. Bailis, A. Davidson, A. Fekete, *et al.* Highly available transactions: Virtues and limitations. *PVLDB*, 7(3):181–192, 2013.

[3] J. Baker, C. Bond, J. C. Corbett, and J. J. Furman, A. Khorlin, J. Larson, J. Leon, Y. Li, A. Lloyd, and V. Yushprakh. Megastore: Providing scalable, highly available storage for interactive services. In *CIDR*, pp. 223–234, 2011.

[4] H. Berenson, P. Bernstein, J. Gray, *et al.* A critique of ANSI SQL isolation levels. *SIGMOD Rec.*, 24(2):1–10, 1995.

[5] P. A. Bernstein, S. Das, B. Ding, *et al.* Optimizing optimistic concurrency control for tree-structured, log-structured databases. In *SIGMOD*, pp. 1295–1309, 2015.

[6] P. A. Bernstein and N. Goodman. Concurrency control in distributed database systems. *ACM Comput. Surv.*, 13(2):185–221, 1981.

[7] C. Binnig, S. Hildenbrand, *et al.* Distributed snapshot isolation: Global transactions pay globally, local transactions pay locally. *VLDB J.*, 23(6):987–1011, 2014.

[8] M. A. Bornea, O. Hodson, S. Elnikety, and A. Fekete. One-copy serializability with snapshot isolation under the hood. In *ICDE*, pp. 625–636, 2011.

[9] E. A. Brewer. Towards robust distributed systems (abstract). In *PODC*, pp. 7–7, 2000.

[10] M. Burrows. The chubby lock service for loosely-coupled distributed systems. In *OSDI*, pp. 335–350, 2006.

[11] C. Mohan *et al.* Aries: A transaction recovery method supporting fine-granularity locking and partial rollbacks using write-ahead logging. *TODS*, 1992.

[12] M. Cao, M. Zhang, A. Sengupta, and M. D. Bond. Drinking from both glasses: combining pessimistic and optimistic tracking of cross-thread dependences. In *PPOPP*, 20:1–20:13. ACM, 2016.

[13] R. Cattell. Scalable sql and nosql data stores. In *ACM SIGMOD Record*, Volume 39, pp. 12–27, 2010.

[14] P. Chairunnanda, K. Daudjee, and T. M. Özsu. ConfluxDB: Multi-master replication for partitioned snapshot isolation databases. In *VLDB*, pp. 947–958, 2014.

[15] T. D. Chandra, R. Griesemer, and J. Redstone. Paxos made live: An engineering perspective. In *Proc. of the Twenty-Sixth Annual ACM Symposium on Principles of Distributed Computing*, pp. 398–407, ACM, 2007.

[16] W. contributors. Apache kafka—wikipedia, the free encyclopedia, 2018. [Online; accessed on 10 April 2018].

[17] B. F. Cooper, A. Silberstein, E. Tam, R. Ramakrishnan, and R. Sears. Benchmarking cloud serving systems with YCSB. In *Proc. of the 1st ACM symposium on Cloud computing*, pp. 143–154. ACM, 2010.

[18] J. C. Corbett, J. Dean, M. Epstein, A. Fikes, C. Frost, J. J. Furman, S. Ghemawat, A. Gubarev, C. Heiser, P. Hochschild, *et al.* Spanner: Googles globally distributed database. *TOCS*, 31(3):8, 2013.

[19] T. Council. tpc-c benchmark, revision 5.11, 2010.

[20] K. Daudjee and K. Salem. Lazy database replication with snapshot isolation. In *VLDB*, pp. 715–726, 2006.

[21] B. D. de Dinechin, R. Ayrignac, P.-E. Beaucamps, P. Couvert, B. Ganne, P. G. de Massas, F. Jacquet, S. Jones, N. M. Chaisemartin, F. Riss, *et al.* A clustered manycore processor architecture for embedded and accelerated applications. In *HPEC*, pp. 1–6, 2013.

[22] G. DeCandia, D. Hastorun, M. Jampani, G. Kakulapati, A. Lakshman, A. Pilchin, S. Sivasubramanian, P. Vosshall, and W. Vogels. Dynamo: Amazon's highly available key-value store. In *SOSP*, pp. 205–220. ACM, 2007.

[23] I. Delchev. Linux traffic control. In *Networks and Distributed Systems Seminar, International University Bremen*, Spring, 2006.

[24] C. Diaconu, C. Freedman, E. Ismert, P.-Å. Larson, P. Mittal, R. Stonecipher, N. Verma, and M. Zwilling. Hekaton: SQL server's memory-optimized OLTP engine. In *SIGMOD*, pp. 1243–1254, ACM, 2013.

[25] D. Ongaro and J. K. Ousterhout. In search of an understandable consensus algorithm. In *Proc. ATC14, USENIX Annual Technical Conference*, pp. 305–319, 2014.

[26] S. Elnikety, W. Zwaenepoel, and F. Pedone. Database replication using generalized snapshot isolation. In *SRDS*, pp. 73–84. IEEE Computer Society, 2005.

[27] F. Färber, S. K. Cha, J. Primsch, C. Bornhövd, S. Sigg, and W. Lehner. Sap hana database: Data management for modern business applications. *SIGMOD*, 40(4):45–51, 2012.

[28] S. Gilbert and N. A. Lynch. Brewer's conjecture and the feasibility of consistent, available, partition-tolerant web services. *SIGACT News*, 33(2):51–59, 2002.

[29] J. Gray. Notes on data base operating systems. In *Operating Systems*, 1978.

[30] J. Gray, P. Helland, P. E. O'Neil, and D. E. Shasha. The dangers of replication and a solution. In *SIGMOD Conference*, pp. 173–182. ACM Press, 1996.

[31] J. N. Gray, R. A. Lorie, and G. R. Putzolu. Granularity of locks in a shared data base. In *VLDB*, pp. 428–451. ACM, 1975.

[32] M. Grund, J. Krüger, H. Plattner, *et al.* Hyrise: A main memory hybrid storage engine. In *Proc. VLDB Endow.*, 4(2):105–116, 2010.

[33] T. Haerder and A. Reuter. Principles of transaction-oriented database recovery. *ACM Comput. Surv.*, 15(4):287–317, 1983.

[34] T. Härder. Observations on optimistic concurrency control schemes. *Inf. Syst.*, 9(2):111–120, 1984.

[35] S. Harizopoulos, D. J. Abadi, S. Madden, and M. Stonebraker. Oltp through the looking glass, and what we found there. In *SIGMOD*, pp. 981–992. ACM, 2008.

[36] C. Hong, D. Zhou, M. Yang, C. Kuo, L. Zhang, and L. Zhou. Kuafu: Closing the parallelism gap in database replication. In *ICDE*, 2013.

[37] H. Howard. ARC: Analysis of Raft Consensus. *Technical Report*, 2014.

[38] P. Hunt, M. Konar, F. P. Junqueira, and B. Reed. Zookeeper: Wait-free coordination for internet-scale systems. In *USENIX Annual Technical Conference*, Volume 8, USENIX Association, Boston, MA, USA, 2010.

[39] R. Johnson, I. Pandis, and A. Ailamaki. Improving oltp scalability using speculative lock inheritance. In *Proc. VLDB Endow.*, pp. 479–489.

[40] R. Johnson, I. Pandis, N. Hardavellas, A. Ailamaki, and B. Falsafi. Shore-mt: A scalable storage manager for the multicore era. In *EDBT*, pp. 24–35. ACM, 2009.

[41] J. W. Josten, C. Mohan, I. Narang, and J. Z. Teng. Db2's use of the coupling facility for data sharing. *IBM Systems Journal*, 36(2):327–351, 1997.

[42] H. Jung, H. Han, A. Fekete, G. Heiser, and H. Y. Yeom. A scalable lock manager for multicores. *ACM Trans. Database Syst.*, 29:1–29:29.

[43] H. Jung, H. Han, A. Fekete, and U. Rhm. Serializable snapshot isolation for replicated databases in high-update scenarios. In *VLDB*, pp. 783–794, 2011.

[44] Junqueira *et al.* Zab: High-performance broadcast for primary-backup systems. In *DSN*, 2011.

[45] R. Kallman, H. Kimura, J. Natkins, A. Pavlo, A. Rasin, S. Zdonik, E. P. Jones, S. Madden, M. Stonebraker, Y. Zhang, *et al.* H-store: A high-performance, distributed main memory transaction processing system. *VLDB*, pp. 1496–1499, 2008.

[46] B. Kemme and G. Alonso. A suite of database replication protocols based on group communication primitives. In *ICDCS*, pp. 156–163, 1998.

[47] B. Kemme and G. Alonso. Don't be lazy, be consistent: Postgres-r, a new way to implement database replication. In *VLDB*, pp. 134–143, 2000.

[48] B. Kemme and G. Alonso. Database replication: A tale of research across communities. *PVLDB*, 3(1):5–12, 2010.

[49] A. Kemper and T. Neumann. Hyper: A hybrid oltp&olap main memory database system based on virtual memory snapshots. In *ICDE*, pp. 195–206. IEEE, 2011.

[50] K. Kim, T. Wang, R. Johnson, and I. Pandis. Ermia: Fast memory-optimized database system for heterogeneous workloads. *SIGMOD*, 10(3):10–2, 2016.

[51] J. Kończak, N. F. de Sousa Santos, T. Żurkowski, P. T. Wojciechowski, and A. Schiper. Jpaxos: State machine replication based on the paxos protocol. *Technical Report*, 2011.

[52] T. Kraska, G. Pang, M. J. Franklin, S. Madden, and A. Fekete. Mdcc: Multi-data center consistency. In *EuroSys*, 2013.

[53] H. T. Kung and J. T. Robinson. On optimistic methods for concurrency control. *ACM Trans. Database Syst.*, 6(2):213–226, 1981.

[54] L. Lamport. The part-time parliament. *TOCS*, 16(2):133–169, 1998.

[55] L. Lamport. Paxos made simple. *ACM SIGACT News*, 32(4):18–25, 2001.

[56] P.-A. Larson, S. Blanas, C. Diaconu, *et al.* High-performance concurrency control mechanisms for main-memory databases. In *Proc. VLDB Endow.*, 5(4):298–309, 2011.

[57] J. Lee, Y. S. Kwon, F. Färber, and E. A. Muehle. Sap hana distributed in-memory database system: Transaction, session, and metadata management. In *ICDE*, pp. 1165–1173, 2013.

[58] J. Lee, S. Moon, K. H. Kim, D. H. Kim, S. K. Cha, W. Han, C. G. Park, H. J. Na, and J. Lee. Parallel replication across formats in SAP HANA for scaling out mixed OLTP/OLAP workloads. *PVLDB*, 10(12):1598–1609, 2017.

[59] J. Levandoski, D. Lomet, S. Sengupta, R. Stutsman, and R. Wang. Multi-version range concurrency control in deuteronomy. *VLDB*, 8(13):2146–2157, 2015.

[60] W. Lin, M. Yang, L. Zhang, and L. Zhou. PacificA: Replication in log-based distributed storage systems. Technical Report MSR-TR-2008-25, 2008.

[61] Y. Lin, B. Kemme, M. Patiño Martínez, and R. Jiménez-Peris. Middleware based data replication providing snapshot isolation. In *SIGMOD*, pp. 419–430, 2005.

[62] B. Liskov and J. Cowling. Viewstamped replication revisited, 2012.

[63] D. Lomet, A. Fekete, R. Wang, and P. Ward. Multi-version concurrency via timestamp range conflict management. In *ICDE*, pp. 714–725, 2012.

[64] H. Mahmoud, F. Nawab, A. Pucher, D. Agrawal, A. El Abbadi. Low-latency multi-datacenter databases using replicated commit. PVLDB, 6(9): 661–672, 2013.

[65] C. Mohan. Aries/kvl: A key-value locking method for concurrency control of multiaction transactions operating on b-tree indexes. In *VLDB*, pp. 392–405. Morgan Kaufmann Publishers Inc., 1990.

[66] C. Mohan, D. Haderle, B. Lindsay, H. Pirahesh, and P. Schwarz. Aries: A transaction recovery method supporting fine-granularity locking and partial rollbacks using write-ahead logging. *ACM Transactions on Database Systems*, 17:94–162, 1992.

[67] B. Momjian. *PostgreSQL: Introduction and Concepts*, Volume 192. Addison-Wesley New York, 2001.

[68] I. Moraru, D. G. Andersen, and M. Kaminsky. Paxos quorum leases: Fast reads without sacrificing writes. In *SOCC*, pp. 22:1–22:13, 2014.

[69] S. Mu, L. Nelson, W. Lloyd, and J. Li. Consolidating concurrency control and consensus for commits under conflicts. In *OSDI*, pp. 517–532, 2016.

[70] F. Nawab, V. Arora, D. Agrawal, and A. El Abbadi. Minimizing commit latency of transactions in geo-replicated data stores. In *SIGMOD*, 2015.

[71] T. Neumann, T. Mühlbauer, and A. Kemper. Fast serializable multi-version concurrency control for main-memory database systems. In *SIGMOD*, pp. 677–689. ACM, 2015.

[72] B. M. Oki and B. H. Liskov. Viewstamped replication: A new primary copy method to support highly-available distributed systems. In *PODC*. ACM, 1988.

[73] D. Ongaro and J. K. Ousterhout. In search of an understandable consensus algorithm. In *USENIX Annual Technical Conference*, pp. 305–319. USENIX Association, 2014.

[74] F. Özcan, Y. Tian, and P. Tözün. Hybrid transactional/analytical processing: A survey. In *SIGMOD Conference*, pp. 1771–1775. ACM, 2017.

[75] A. Pavlo and M. Aslett. What's really new with newsql? *SIGMOD Rec.*, 45(2):45–55, 2016.

[76] F. Pedone, M. Wiesmann, A. Schiper, B. Kemme, and G. Alonso. Understanding replication in databases and distributed systems. In *ICDCS*, pp. 464–474, 2000.

[77] K. Ren, A. Thomson, and D. J. Abadi. Lightweight locking for main memory database systems. *PVLDB*, 6(2):145–156, 2012.

[78] H. Plattner. The impact of columnar in-memory databases on enterprise systems: Implications of eliminating transaction-maintained aggregates. *VLDB*, 7(13):1722–1729, 2014.

[79] D. R. K. Ports and K. Grittner. Serializable snapshot isolation in postgresql. In *Proc. VLDB Endow.*, 5(12):1850–1861, Aug. 2012.

[80] D. Qin, A. Goel, and A. D. Brown. Scalable replay-based replication for fast databases. *PVLDB*, 10(13):2025–2036, 2017.

[81] C. Ramey. Tile-gx100 manycore processor: Acceleration interfaces and architecture. In *2011 IEEE, Hot Chips 23 Symposium (HCS)*, pp. 1–21, IEEE, 2011.

[82] J. Rao, E. J. Shekita, and S. Tata. Using paxos to build a scalable, consistent, and highly available datastore. *PVLDB*, 4(4):243–254, 2011.

[83] M. Reimer. Solving the phantom problem by predicative optimistic concurrency control. In *VLDB*, pp. 81–88. Morgan Kaufmann Publishers Inc., 1983.

[84] K. Ren, J. M. Faleiro, and D. J. Abadi. Design principles for scaling multi-core oltp under high contention. In *SIGMOD*, pp. 1583–1598. ACM, 2016.

[85] N. Santos and A. Schiper. Tuning paxos for high-throughput with batching and pipelining. In *13th International Conference Distributed Computing and Networking*, pp. 153–167, 2012.

[86] F. B. Schneider. Implementing fault-tolerant services using the state machine approach: A tutorial. *CSUR*, 22(4):299–319, 1990.

[87] V. Sikka, F. Färber, W. Lehner, *et al.* Efficient transaction processing in sap hana database: The end of a column store myth. In *SIGMOD*, pp. 731–742, 2012.

[88] M. Stonebraker. Concurrency control and consistency of multiple copies of data in distributed ingres. *IEEE Transactions on Software Engineering*, (3):188–194, 1979.

[89] M. Stonebraker, S. Madden, D. J. Abadi, S. Harizopoulos, N. Hachem, and P. Helland. The end of an architectural era: (it's time for a complete rewrite). In *VLDB*, pp. 1150–1160. VLDB Endowment, 2007.

[90] D. Tang and A. J. Elmore. Toward coordination-free and reconfigurable mixed concurrency control. In *2018 USENIX Annual Technical Conference (USENIX ATC 18)*, Boston, MA, 2018.

[91] D. Tang, H. Jiang, and A. J. Elmore. Adaptive concurrency control: Despite the looking glass, one concurrency control does not fit all. In *CIDR*, Volume 2, p. 1, 2017.

[92] T. Zhu. Towards a shared-everything database on distributed log-structured storage. In *ATC*, 2018.

[93] S. Tu, W. Zheng, E. Kohler, B. Liskov, and S. Madden. Speedy transactions in multicore in-memory databases. In *SOSP*, pp. 18–32. ACM, 2013.

[94] R. Van Renesse and D. Altinbuken. Paxos made moderately complex. *ACM Comput. Surv.*, 2015.

[95] R. van Renesse, N. Schiper, and F. B. Schneider. Vive la différence: Paxos vs. viewstamped replication vs. zab. *IEEE Trans. Dependable Sec. Comput.*, 12(4):472–484, 2015.

[96] T. Wang and H. Kimura. Mostly-optimistic concurrency control for highly contended dynamic workloads on a thousand cores. *VLDB*, 10(2):49–60, 2016.

[97] M. Wiesmann, F. Pedone, A. Schiper, B. Kemme, and G. Alonso. Database replication techniques: A three parameter classification. In *Reliable Distributed Systems, 2000. SRDS-2000. In Proc. The 19th IEEE Symposium on*, pp. 206–215. IEEE, 2000.

[98] M. Wiesmann and A. Schiper. Comparison of database replication techniques based on total order broadcast. *TKDE*, 17(4):551–566, 2005.

[99] Y. Wu, J. Arulraj, J. Lin *et al.* An empirical evaluation of in-memory multi-version concurrency control. In *Proc. VLDB Endow.*, 10(7):781–792, 2017.

[100] Y. Wu, C.-Y. Chan, and K.-L. Tan. Transaction healing: Scaling optimistic concurrency control on multicores. In *Proc. of the 2016 International Conference on Management of Data*, SIGMOD, pp. 1689–1704, 2016.

[101] C. Yan and A. Cheung. Leveraging lock contention to improve oltp application performance. In *Proc. VLDB Endow.*, pp. 444–455.

[102] X. Yu, G. Bezerra, A. Pavlo, S. Devadas, and M. Stonebraker. Staring into the abyss: An evaluation of concurrency control with one thousand cores. *VLDB*, pp. 209–220, 2014.

[103] X. Yu, A. Pavlo, D. Sanchez, and S. Devadas. Tictoc: Time traveling optimistic concurrency control. In *SIGMOD*, Volume 8, pp. 209–220. VLDB Endowment, 2016.

[104] X. Yu, S. Zhu, J. Kaashoek, A. Pavlo, and S. Devadas. Taurus: A parallel transaction recovery method based on fine-granularity dependency tracking.

[105] Y. Yuan, K. Wang, R. Lee, X. Ding, J. Xing, S. Blanas, and X. Zhang. Bcc: Reducing false aborts in optimistic concurrency control with low cost for in-memory databases. *VLDB*, 9(6):504–515, 2016.

[106] I. Zhang, N. K. Sharma, A. Szekeres *et al.* Building consistent transactions with inconsistent replication. In *SOSP*, pp. 263–278. ACM, 2015.

[107] T. Zhang, A. Tomasic, Y. Sheng, and A. Pavlo. Performance of oltp via intelligent scheduling. In *34th IEEE International Conference on Data Engineering, ICDE 2018, Paris, France, April 19-22, 2018*, pp. 1288–1291, 2018.

[108] J. Zheng, Q. Lin, J. Xu, C. Wei, C. Zeng, P. Yang, and Y. Zhang. Paxosstore: High-availability storage made practical in wechat. *Proc. VLDB Endow.*, 2017.

[109] W. Zheng, S. Tu, E. Kohler, and B. Liskov. Fast databases with fast durability and recovery through multicore parallelism. In *OSDI*, pp. 465–477, 2014.

Index

Index

write request, 18
write set, 22
write skew problem, 7
write-ahead logging, 8
write-intensive micro-benchmark, 107
write-intensive operations, 84
write-intensive workload, 35, 60, 108
write/read ratios, 110

Y

YCSB benchmark, 51, 83, 107, 137

Z

zab protocol, 143
Zipfian distribution, 51

East China Normal University Scientific Reports
Subseries on Data Science and Engineering

Published (continued from page ii)